The Gospel of Thomas

The Gospel of Thomas

Annotated & Explained

Translation & annotation
by Stevan Davies

DARTON·LONGMAN+TODD

First published in Great Britain in 2003 by
Darton, Longman and Todd Ltd
1 Spencer Court
140–142 Wandsworth High Street
London SW18 4JJ

First published in the USA in 2002 by
SkyLight Paths Publishing, a division of LongHill Partners, Inc.
Sunset Farm Offices, Route 4, P.O. Box 237
Woodstock, VT 05091

Reprinted 2004, (twice)

The photograph on p. vi appears courtesy of the Institute for Antiquity and Christianity, Claremont, California.

ISBN 0–232–52501–3

A catalogue record for this book is available from the British Library.

Text design by Chelsea Cloeter
Printed and bound in Great Britain by
CPI Bath

To Sally Augusta Watkins Davies

Title page of the original Coptic Gospel of Thomas.

Contents

About the Gospel of Thomas

In 1968 or so I was an undergraduate at Duke University, wandering around in the Divinity School library stacks, when I came upon a translation of the Gospel of Thomas. I read it on the spot; it really isn't very long. I remember my first impression to this day, which was that the sayings of Jesus in Thomas's Gospel seemed altogether more pleasant than the sayings in the canonical texts. Lacking was any emphasis on judgment or on the coming end of this world. The canonical set of sayings, those with which we are familiar, frequently refer to the imminent future end of this world and the arrival of the Kingdom of Heaven. The Gospel of Thomas, though, features sayings that emphasize valuing the present, sayings that assert that the Kingdom of Heaven is here now and that it has been here since the beginning of the world. Accordingly, Thomas's sayings lack predictions of destruction, images of trial and judgment, warnings to beware the imminent arrival of the day of doom. Instead, they urge self-knowledge, contemplation of the nature of this world now, and reflection on the beginning of all things. I, and many other people, would prefer to think that Jesus spoke in the manner of the Gospel of Thomas rather than in the manner of the church's gospels, but we all must bear in mind that our preferences are irrelevant to the determination of historical fact.

Naturally the question arises whether Thomas's Gospel is generally representative of the authentic words of Jesus or whether it was invented by a group of Christians intending to push their own agenda by using Jesus' authority. It has become clear to me, as it is to most people who study the matter, that every one of the Christian documents we have from the first centuries was developed by Christians intending to promote their own agendas, usually by directly or indirectly attributing their ideas to

Jesus. It has become obvious to me, as to many others, that the gospels of the canonical New Testament, insofar as they have sayings of the sort that the Gospel of Thomas contains (John's Gospel does not; the other three do), are dependent on earlier documents for those sayings. Matthew and Luke depend almost entirely on Mark's Gospel and on a now lost list of sayings that scholars call Q. Mark, in turn, is dependent on earlier sources (one of which, I have argued in a two-part essay in the journal *Neotestamentica* [1996], may be the Gospel of Thomas). We have no reliable objective source of Jesus' teachings, only a few texts wherein people express their own ideas through sayings attributed to Jesus. It is entirely possible that some of those ideas were shared by Jesus himself, but simply because a view is attributed to him in a text does not guarantee that it is his own view.

There appear to have been at least two divergent streams of Christian tradition in the first century, streams that made use of the kinds of sayings we find in the Gospel of Thomas and in the canonical gospels. It is very likely, if not certain, that at least one of them did not originate with Jesus himself. The two streams flow in opposite directions: one toward the past, urging people to find the Kingdom here now, telling people to understand it as having originated during the days of Genesis 1. It urges self-reliance and has as a key injunction "seek and find," insisting that the Kingdom results from inner self-discovery. This stream of tradition is found in the Gospel of Thomas. The other stream flows toward the future—into a time when this world will be radically transformed from the outside when God acts to send the Kingdom down upon it. People must prepare by revising their relationships to other people and by successfully passing a judgment by trial. But, fundamentally, people are not to be self-reliant but to wait faithfully for unearned grace to save them. That stream originates in Paul and Mark and in the revisions of Mark's Gospel that we call the Gospels of Matthew and Luke.

The heresy-hunting proponents of Christian orthodoxy not only selected the texts that they insisted must be regarded as the authentic voice of Jesus—the texts we find in the New Testament—but also systematically sought to destroy every other text. Until the discovery of the Gospel of Thomas, that effort had succeeded remarkably well. Thomas, though, gives us another view. It opens up the possibility that the orthodox future-oriented "eschatological" Christianity that was later chosen to represent Jesus' views was not his own perspective but that of the one victorious group among all of the first-century groups that taught in his name.

In 1983 I published a book about the Gospel of Thomas entitled *The Gospel of Thomas and Christian Wisdom* (New York: Seabury Press). As the title indicates, most of the book was an argument that Thomas should be considered primarily to have originated from the wisdom tradition of Judaism—a tradition that can be found in the Book of Proverbs and in other Jewish texts of the centuries just before the birth of Christianity. Both in the Gospel of Thomas and in the canonical gospels, we can see evidence that Jesus was thought to have embodied the characteristics of the Wisdom of God, who had been regarded for some time by some Jewish thinkers as a semi-independent supernatural person through whom God acted.

In part, *The Gospel of Thomas and Christian Wisdom* was written to argue against an idea that still seems to have its supporters. That idea is that the Gospel of Thomas is a Gnostic gospel put together by heretics of the third century out of scraps of material they mined from the canonical scriptures. Those Gnostics are said to be people who believe in a demonic god ruling this earth through other gods called archons, who made this earth in order to trap human souls. They, the demonic archons, require souls for their own survival, and they develop false myths, equated with Judaism, to keep people ignorant of the truth. The truth, though, is that humans originate from a God from the highest level of the universe, and once humans realize that this is the truth, they can ascend through the lower archon-riddled spheres to the highest world above. Christian Gnostics believed that the fundamental salvation brought by Jesus was to inform people of their entrapment, and of the complicated sequence of events that led to that entrapment, and so give them saving knowledge that would enable them to escape. Because it was a religion focused on knowledge, *gnosis* in Greek, it came to be known as Gnostic.

None of this interesting and complicated Gnostic theorizing is found anywhere in the Gospel of Thomas. In fact, with its emphasis on the presence of the Kingdom of Heaven within the world now, Thomas is, if anything, anti-Gnostic, for Gnosticism emphatically insisted that the Kingdom of Heaven is to be found in the highest sphere above this world and certainly not here among the archons. The reason why Thomas has been called Gnostic was, I believe, twofold. First, it is a fact that when Thomas was discovered in 1945, it was bound together in a library of writings that are unquestionably Gnostic. Logic was applied as follows: if some of the texts are Gnostic, they must all be, and since Thomas is one of them, it must be Gnostic too—even in the absence of significant evidence showing that it is. Second, Gnostic Christianity has been the most virulently hated form of heresy in Christian history, subject to violent intellectual and physical attack from the second century on. To say that a text is Gnostic is to say, in effect, not only that it is irrelevant to anything of significance to Christians but that it should be completely ignored.

The discovery of the Gospel of Thomas threatened conservative Christian scholars in a way they had never been threatened before. Whether or not the canon of scriptures is to be considered inerrantly true is a matter of faith. Whether they are the only significant source of information about Jesus is not a matter of faith but a matter of historical judgment. Until the discovery of the Gospel of Thomas, however, no scholars claimed that any texts from the ancient world contained any significant amount of information about Jesus. Accordingly, only the canonical scriptures were useful in the effort to learn about him and his teachings. With the Gospel of Thomas, a new source appeared for the first time. Thomas's sayings seemed to be at least as early as the New Testament gospels, and their present-oriented self-reflective Christianity had a decent claim to be the teachings of Jesus himself. In my opinion, there has been a considerable uncoordinated effort to make the Gospel of Thomas go away, to have it become completely intellectually irrelevant. One way to do that is to declare that it is Gnostic, hence heretical, hence late in date, dependent on the scriptures for any of its information, and, most important, no threat to the established view.

The translation included in the present book was constructed by the use of the original Coptic and Greek with considerable assistance drawn from Michael Grondin's interlinear translation (http://www.geocities.com/Athens/9068/) and with reference to the following translations of the Gospel of Thomas: Thomas Lambdin in *The Nag Hammadi Library in English*, edited by James M. Robinson, third edition (San Francisco: HarperSanFrancisco, 1988); Bentley Layton, *The Gnostic Scriptures* (New York: Doubleday, 1987); Bruce M. Metzger, "The Gospel of Thomas Translated," in *Synoptis Quattour Evangeliorum: Locis parallelis evangeliorum apocryphum et patrum adhibitis*, edited by K. Aland (Stuttgart: Wurttembergische Bibelanstalt, 1964); Marvin Meyer and Stephen Patterson, *Q-Thomas Reader* (Sonoma, Calif.: Polebridge Press, 1990); A. Guillaumont, H. C. Puech, G. Quispel, W. Till, and Y. `Abd al Masih, *The Gospel According to Thomas: Coptic Text Established and Translated* (Leiden/London/New York: E.J. Brill/Collins/Harper, 1959); David R. Cartlidge, *Documents for the Study of the Gospels* (Cleveland: Collins, 1980); Ray Summers, *The Secret Sayings of the Living Jesus* (Waco, Tex.: Word Books, 1968); Jean Doresse, *The Secret Books of the Egyptian Gnostics: An Introduction to the Gnostic Coptic Manuscripts Discovered at Chenoboskion* (New York/London: Viking/Hollis & Carter, 1960).

The present commentary is not intended to be a clear guide to understanding the Gospel of Thomas. One might think that that should be its goal, but, ironically, if one could find a way to make clear unambiguous sense out of Thomas's sayings, one would thereby spoil the document and ruin it for the reader. The Gospel of Thomas is not intended to be easily understood. The text itself declares in its first sentences that the discovery of the correct interpretation of the sayings will lead to immortality, that one who seeks and finds their meaning will be disturbed and astonished. The sayings in Thomas are supposed to be enigmatic, difficult to fathom, and difficult to understand. The reader is supposed to seek their meaning and find their hidden messages.

What, then, is the role of a commentary on the Gospel of Thomas? Even if I did clearly know the secret of the text—and I don't make that claim—the purpose the Gospel of Thomas sets out for itself is to challenge every reader to seek and find its meaning. Therefore its secret must be actively sought. To learn the full meaning of the Gospel of Thomas from someone else would defeat the self-proclaimed intention of the document to present a challenge of interpretation that will potentially lead to eternal life. The role of a commentary is, then, to offer suggestions, share observations, and participate in a reader's seeking, but not to do the finding for the reader. This commentary will give you new ways of looking at these sayings of Jesus and open up directions of inquiry for you. But you ultimately must seek what you will find. No one else can do that for you.

Introduction

For those interested in Jesus of Nazareth and the origins of Christianity, the Gospel of Thomas is the most important manuscript discovery ever made. Apart from the canonical scriptures and a few scattered sayings, the Gospel of Thomas is our only historically valuable source for the teachings of Jesus. Although it has been available in European languages since the 1950s, it is still subject to intense scrutiny and debate by biblical scholars. The Gospel of Thomas is roughly the same age as the canonical New Testament gospels, but it contains sayings of Jesus that present very different views on religion and on the nature of humanity and salvation, and it thereby raises the question whether the New Testament's version of Jesus' teachings is entirely accurate and complete.

In late 1945, an Egyptian peasant named Mohammed Ali al-Samman Mohammad Khalifa rode his camel to the base of a cliff, hoping to find fertilizer to sell in the nearby village of Nag Hammadi. He found, instead, a large sealed pottery jar buried in the sand. He feared it might contain a genie that would haunt or attack him, and he hoped it might contain a treasure. Gathering his courage, he smashed open the jar and discovered only a collection of twelve old books. Suspecting that they might have value on the antiquities market, he kept the books and eventually sold them for a small sum. The books gradually came into the hands of scholars in Cairo, Europe, and America. Today those books are known as the Nag Hammadi library, a collection that is generally considered to be the most important archaeological discovery of the twentieth century for research into the New Testament and early Christianity. The Nag Hammadi library contains the Gospel of Philip, the Gospel of Truth, the Gospel of the Egyptians, the Secret Book of James, the Secret Book of

John, and many other fascinating texts ranging in date from the second through the middle of the fourth centuries A.D. The twelve books contain fifty-two texts altogether, forty of which were previously unknown to scholarship.

Of all the Nag Hammadi texts, by far the most significant is the Gospel of Thomas. Scholars knew of the existence of the Gospel of Thomas before the Nag Hammadi discovery because it was mentioned in the works of Hippolytus, a third-century church father. At the end of the nineteenth century, fragments of the Gospel of Thomas in the Greek language were found in the rich Egyptian archaeological site known as Oxyrhynchus, a discovery that excited great interest among New Testament scholars because the fragments contained sayings of Jesus that were familiar from the New Testament but appeared to have been transcribed from independent oral tradition and therefore were a new source for the teachings of Jesus.

When the full Gospel of Thomas came to light in the Nag Hammadi Library fifty years later, it was excitedly greeted as if it were an old friend. Scholars immediately saw that they now possessed the full version of what they had known before only in fragments. The version of the Gospel of Thomas found at Nag Hammadi, like all the texts in that collection, was written in Coptic, the language of ancient Egypt put into an alphabet derived from (but not entirely identical to) the Greek alphabet. The newly found text was not an original Coptic composition but a translation of a Greek original, the same Greek sayings list that had been found in fragments at Oxyrhynchus.

The Gospel of Thomas contains roughly 150 sayings attributed to Jesus, about half of which are also found in the canonical New Testament gospels of Matthew, Mark, and Luke. It does not contain sayings found also in the Gospel of John. For convenience, scholars have numbered the sayings in a standard sequence, almost always basing the numbers on the occurrence of the phrase "Jesus said." By that method the standard list contains 114 sayings, some of which are two or more sayings combined into one. Thomas contains no sustained narrative at all, although it contains a few narrative elements, for example, "a woman in the crowd said to him" (79), "Jesus saw infants being suckled. He said to his disciples..." (22).

The format of the Gospel of Thomas is little more than a disorganized list. The sayings at the very beginning (sayings 1–3) and end (113) may have been deliberately placed in those locations, but the rest of the sayings, despite the efforts of many scholars over the past half century to find order in them, appear to have been haphazardly put together. To some degree, the Gospel of Thomas begins to repeat sayings toward its end, and several times throughout the text, sayings of the same general sort—short sets of proverbs for example, or parables—appear adjacent to one another. Sometimes adjacent sayings share a word or a motif, but otherwise there's no known order to the list. The Gospel of Thomas is about as primitive a form of text as there can be: a simple list with one thing following another in a manner that is much more reminiscent of oral tradition than of literary construction. It appears most likely that the sayings list we call the Gospel of Thomas was transcribed by a scribe on a particular occasion from the word-of-mouth recitations by some people who were trying to remember what they could of what Jesus reportedly had said.

For most people, the Gospel of Thomas's greatest significance arises from the fact that so many of its sayings are similar to sayings in the canonical gospels. This raises the question whether Thomas is a source for the teachings of Jesus independent of the New Testament gospels, or whether it is dependent on those canonical gospels. If the Gospel of Thomas is independent, its sayings were derived from sources other than the New Testament gospels, most probably from oral rather than written sources. If it is dependent, then its sayings were taken from the New Testament. If it is independent, then the Gospel of Thomas gives us a new source for the teachings of Jesus of Nazareth, our first new source for nearly two thousand years and one second in importance only to the biblical books. On the other hand, if the Gospel of Thomas is dependent on the canonical scriptures, then—while it provides some interesting insight into a very early Christian cult—it offers no new information of significance about Jesus of Nazareth.

Those who argue that Thomas is dependent on the canonical gospels for its sayings point to the fact that, according to the most widely held theory of New Testament origins, the Gospel of Mark was revised by Matthew and Luke as they incorporated it into their own gospels. Accordingly, when a word or phrase appears in Matthew or Luke in a passage they have in common with Mark, but that particular word or phrase does not itself appear in Mark, it generally indicates that Matthew or Luke has changed Mark. Now, if the same word shows up in the equivalent saying in Thomas, some find it reasonable to presume that Thomas found the word in Matthew's or Luke's Gospel and therefore took the saying from that existing gospel. Since this happens on a few occasions, some conclude that Thomas must have used Matthew's and Luke's Gospels as a source.

On the other hand, many scholars argue that there are so few hints of dependence by Thomas on Matthew's or Luke's or Mark's Gospels that the hints that do exist can best be explained by the fact that Christian scribes copied and translated Thomas throughout the centuries before it was hidden at Nag Hammadi. The history of the New Testament manuscript tradition shows that the scribes who copied such manuscripts invariably made mistakes, made what they thought were improvements, copied what they remembered a saying to be rather than what a manuscript in front of them said it was, and so forth. In other words, as scribes copied Thomas they did so in light of their own knowledge of the canonical gospels, and the same would be true for whoever it was who translated the Gospel of Thomas from Greek into Coptic. It is only reasonable to presume that their knowledge of the canonical gospels occasionally led them to change Thomas's sayings as they copied them, and as time went on, sayings in copies of the Gospel of Thomas increasingly came to resemble their New Testament counterparts. Therefore, if on a few occasions

Thomas's sayings have words that accord with Matthew's or Luke's version of sayings rather than Mark's version, this does not by any means prove that the Gospel of Thomas is dependent on Matthew's or Luke's Gospels, only that scribes in the chain of copying and translating were familiar with the canonical gospels.

The Gospel of Thomas seems often to contain sayings of Jesus in a less revised state than they are in the canonical gospels. In the words of Professor Helmut Koester of the Harvard Divinity School: "If one considers the form and wording of the individual sayings in comparison with the form in which they are preserved in the New Testament, the Gospel of Thomas almost always appears to have preserved a more original form of the traditional saying or presents versions which are independently based on more original forms. In a few instances where this is not the case, the Coptic translation seems to have been influenced by the translator's knowledge of the New Testament gospels."

Many scholars have noted that Thomas is the most primitive possible form of written tradition, a simple barely organized list, and that to a great extent the sayings in the Gospel of Thomas that do overlap with versions in the canonical gospels show absolutely no sign of having been taken from those gospels. In addition, there is virtually no overlap in the order of the sayings, for virtually none of the sayings in Thomas occur in the same sequence as they do in Matthew or Mark or Luke. All these factors argue for Thomas's independence from the influence of the canonical gospels, as does the fact that the Gospel of Thomas does not contain any reference to the great Christian themes of crucifixion and resurrection, or any reference to Jesus' status as Messiah or Christ, or the stories of him as virgin-born and capable of miraculous actions. One of the most likely reasons for the absence of these concepts is that the Gospel of Thomas was compiled before those Christian themes were fully developed. Significantly, Thomas also lacks the imaginative cosmological speculations typical of later Christian Gnostic texts. It seems to have come into being before those kinds of writings were developed.

The Gospel of Thomas, it now appears, is very likely to be independent of the New Testament's canonical gospels and therefore to be a new source for the teachings of Jesus. Since it is in such a primitive form—the unstructured list—and since it shows no signs of the great themes of Christianity that developed in the early church, and since the forms of the sayings in Thomas are often less developed than they are in the canonical gospels, it stands to reason that Thomas is quite an early text. It may perhaps have been written before 62 A.D., for there is a hint of a date in that period in the Gospel of Thomas itself: saying 12 commends Jesus' brother James to be the leader of the Christian movement after Jesus himself is no longer on earth. James died in the year 62 A.D. It follows that a saying recommending his leadership would probably not have been incorporated into Thomas after that year. Be that as it may, one cannot say for certain when Thomas was written, for, apart from the hint supplied by saying 12, there are no chronological indicators in the text.

There are no clear geographical indicators in the Gospel of Thomas, for it contains no narratives that give us place names. However, we may have one clue in the title of the text itself. In the early days of the Christian movement, different regions claimed different apostles as the founders of their own churches. Mark was said to have founded the church in Egypt, John the church in Greece, Peter the church in Rome, and Thomas the church in Syria. The Acts of Thomas, a late-third-century Syrian pious novel, and the Book of Thomas, which is a fictional fourth-century Syrian dialogue between Thomas and Jesus, testify to a particular Syrian interest in Thomas the apostle. As does the much earlier Gospel of Thomas, those texts refer to "Judas Thomas." Some argue that because of the significance of the apostle Thomas to later Syrian Christianity, the Gospel of Thomas probably comes from Syria. Syria is the northern neighbor of Galilee and had an established Christian community at least by the early 30s A.D. at which time Paul was making his way to Damascus to confront the Christian church there.

Most New Testament scholars find a theory known as the "two-source hypothesis" to be the most convincing way to account for the fact that the Gospels of Matthew, Mark, and Luke are word-for-word identical in the Greek of many passages. The "two-source hypothesis" holds that Matthew and Luke used two texts as principal sources for their own gospels. One of those texts is the narrative we call the Gospel of Mark. The other text is a now lost collection of the sayings of Jesus that German scholarship came to call "the source" or, in German, *Quelle*, or, now quite commonly, just Q. This Q can be reconstructed from the Gospels of Matthew and Luke, for, in the simplest formulation, Q is simply a list of the material that we find in Matthew's and Luke's Gospels that we do not find in Mark's Gospel. Today the two-source hypothesis is so commonly accepted that books are now published discussing Q as though it were a real existing text.

The "two-source hypothesis" was attacked in earlier decades because, for one thing, there was no evidence that Christian communities composed lists of sayings; no list like the hypothetical Q had ever been discovered. But now the discovery of the Gospel of Thomas has confirmed the hypothesis that lists of sayings definitely existed during the earliest times of Christianity.

Today, many scholars of Christian origins will place the reconstructed Q list side by side with the newly discovered Thomas list as the earliest gospels that we have. Q and the Gospel of Thomas are not the same thing. Q, as reconstructed by scholarship, appears to have been somewhat more coherently organized than the Gospel of Thomas and to have begun to take on the form of a narrative of Jesus' life.

Thomas and Q are significantly different in terms of the points of view their contents advocate. The Q list, through its selection of sayings, presents Jesus as a man who taught that the Kingdom of God would come in the very near future. Only a few will be allowed into the Kingdom when it comes, but everyone will see it arrive "like a lightning flash." To be allowed into the Kingdom, one must begin to behave appropriately; one must "do unto others as you would have God do unto you." As you forgive others God will forgive you; as you judge others God will judge you. This combination of future orientation and judgment based on moral behavior has characterized much of Christianity to this day. Like Thomas, however, Q shows no significant interest in the motif of crucifixion and resurrection or salvation through grace and faith.

The sayings in the Gospel of Thomas present a startling contrast to this point of view. Thomas also speaks of the Kingdom of the Father, but here we find that the Kingdom already exists on the earth and has existed since the very beginning of time. When Jesus is asked about the coming of the Kingdom in Thomas, he invariably replies that the Kingdom is here now; it is right in front of your face, even though people usually do not see it. The Gospel of Thomas implies that the Kingdom has always been present, ever since the first days of creation. But its presence is now hidden from almost everyone. One might summarize the Gospel of Thomas as saying: "Find the Kingdom that is right here." Some have compared this perspective to such Eastern philosophies as Zen Buddhism. Few religious texts in the West insist that perfection exists on this earth now, if you can find it. Rather, the Western religions generally place perfection in the heavens and in the future. Thomas's Gospel presents a very different view.

The idea that the Kingdom is already here, but usually undiscovered, leads logically to the idea that a person's greatest accomplishment would be to find the Kingdom. The motif "seek and ye shall find" occurs throughout the Gospel of Thomas. If people are inherently able to find the Kingdom, they nevertheless will need guidance as to how to do it. That is the purpose of the Gospel of Thomas: to give directions toward finding the Kingdom. Those directions, however, are presented in a deliberately obscure fashion. The directions come as riddles, as sayings of Jesus that need to be deciphered in order to be understood. The Gospel of Thomas sets itself up as a model for spiritual endeavor. Just as people should approach its sayings as having deeper hidden meaning that is not immediately apparent, so also should they perceive the world as having deeper hidden meaning.

Thomas conveys a very positive view of human nature. People are capable of discovering hidden truth, both in the world and within themselves. Indeed, as the Kingdom is already in the world, so it is already inside of people. Accordingly, if you know yourself properly, you know the Kingdom of God. While Thomas has some sayings that point to a moral dimension for human life, its overall approach is structured in terms of self-knowledge and discovery.

Significantly, there is no place in the Gospel of Thomas for the great themes of sin and salvation as they are found in the canonical New Testament. The human problem is not defined as separation from God as a result of one's moral failings or the mythical failings of Adam, nor is the solution presented in terms of faith in the death of Christ for sins, or in reference to the resurrection of Christ. Those themes are absent.

Thomas gives us a whole new kind of first-century Christianity. It has been called a Gnostic Christianity; *gnosis* is the Greek word for knowledge, and the term *gnostic* has *gnosis* at its root. A wide variety of Gnostic Christianities emerged during the second century with increasingly complicated and, to us, bizarre views of the creation and history of the cosmos. Most of the Nag Hammadi collection of texts can be categorized as Christian Gnostic. The Gospel of Thomas, however, is not properly called Gnostic because it completely lacks interest in the history of the cosmos that the later Gnostic texts find so fascinating. Still, Thomas does advocate a point of view that Gnostic Christians also held: that knowledge of the divine and knowledge of oneself are inseparable.

Those who find the Gospel of Thomas interesting often wonder why it is not in the Bible alongside the Gospels of Matthew, Mark, Luke, and John. Unfortunately, there is no good answer to that question because we do not know how the canonical gospels came to be selected in the first place. Around the year 180 A.D., Irenaeus, the bishop of Lyon in what is now France, argued that there should be only the four gospels of the New

Testament in the church's official collection. He assumed that his orthodox readers were already well aware that there are four and only four. But how the decision for four and not three and not five came to pass, we do not know. One cannot assume that Thomas was deliberately excluded from the canon of scripture because we have no idea whether those who decided on the canonical four had ever even heard of the Gospel of Thomas. Thomas may have circulated extensively in the Eastern churches, from Syria to Egypt, and yet have remained almost unknown to churches in the West.

The Gospel of Thomas appears at first to be only a sporadic collection of disconnected sayings. But examination of those sayings one by one can lead to a more comprehensive vision of what the compilers of the text intended to communicate. The Gospel must be read carefully, saying by saying, and one must allow the meaning of the whole to build gradually. If one does this successfully, and if one comes to find the right interpretation of the sayings in Thomas, then, the text promises, one "will not taste death."

Cast of Characters

Jesus: Thomas claims to record the sayings of the historical Jesus: "the living Jesus" rather than the risen Jesus. Jesus came in the flesh and instructed people so that they might have a correct comprehension of themselves and the world. While saying 77 may identify Jesus with the persisting light of creation, saying 24 states that there is light within human beings as well.

Disciples: The disciples in Thomas, with the exception of James (who is perhaps not a disciple) in 12 and Thomas in 13, are examples of people who misunderstand (18, 22, 37, 51, 52, 113, 114). They question Jesus about his own nature and about the world's future. He redirects their inquiries toward their own present situation.

James: Mentioned only in saying 12, James is probably the brother of Jesus, whom Jesus presents, with a traditional praise formula, as his successor as leader of the movement.

Thomas: The supposed scribe who wrote down these sayings. Thomas, according to saying 13, became equivalent to Jesus and received sayings the other disciples would find blasphemous.

Peter: In sayings 13 and 114, Peter is shown to be in error. In 13 he declares Jesus to be a righteous messenger (Greek *aggelos*); in 114 he fails to understand that Mary can be transformed so as to be worthy.

Matthew: In saying 13, Matthew erroneously declares Jesus to be a wise man, a philosopher (Greek *philosophos*). Conceivably, Matthew's and Peter's opinions in 13 reflect the views of rival Christian sects that traced their origins to those individuals.

Mary or Miriam: A person by this name questions Jesus in saying 21 and is repudiated by Peter in saying 114. If Peter desires that she "leave us," she is a member of an inner group of disciples, although inferior to others in that she is not yet "male." But see the comment on saying 114 below. With which Mary in the Christian tradition one should identify this figure is unknown.

Salome: She is mentioned only in saying 61, which is quite obscure. Salome is evidently Jesus' hostess and perhaps also his disciple. She is also mentioned by Mark in 15:40 and 16:1 as one of the women who discovered Jesus' empty tomb.

The Gospel of Thomas

1 The "hidden-ness" of the sayings has to do with their enigmatic character. The meaning of these sayings is hidden within them as, for example, leaven is hidden in dough (saying 96) or a treasure might be hidden in a field (saying 109). The Gospel of Thomas is optimistic that what is hidden will be revealed (sayings 5, 6, 108). These are not sayings that were supposed to be kept secret from other people, though, for roughly half of them are found in Matthew's and Mark's and Luke's Gospels, so it's likely that they were all commonly known and widely circulated.

2 Immortality is said to be the reward of anyone who successfully decodes Thomas's enigmatic sayings. The correct interpretation of the sayings is not the final goal but the means to the goal, the discovery of the Kingdom of Heaven. Thomas's Gospel is an exercise book, a list of riddles for decoding. The secret lies not in the final answers but in the effort to find the answers.

3 This Gospel's Christianity is not based on grace, on salvation given as a gift by God, but on active individual effort. Successful effort will be accompanied by strong emotions, for whatever is to be found will be disturbing and then astonishing. Thomas often uses the motif of "seek and find" (for example, in sayings 2, 38, 92, 94), but it is never made clear exactly what it is one is seeking. As did God's Image in Genesis 1:28, human beings will come some day to reign over everything within the worlds that they find within themselves.

Sayings of the Gospel of Thomas

Incipit: These are the hidden sayings that the living Jesus spoke and that Didymus Judas Thomas wrote down.[1]

1 And he said: Whoever finds the correct interpretation of these sayings will never die.[2]

2 Jesus said: The seeker should not stop until he finds. When he does find, he will be disturbed. After having been disturbed, he will be astonished. Then he will reign over everything.[3]

4 Having introduced the principle that the Kingdom is to be sought and found, the Gospel of Thomas parodies two ideas attributed to rival leaders. The Kingdom is not to be found across the sea, and it is not up in the sky. Even today, many people will point to the sky if asked where heaven is to be found. But this saying makes fun of such an idea. The Kingdom is within you, as Luke's Gospel also says (17:20–21). And yet it is also outside. Thomas is a spiritual Gospel, yet it points out to the world of nature and to the realm of all creation instead of pointing only back toward the reader.

5 The idea that self-knowledge is a road to salvation is perhaps as old as philosophy itself. Its most famous occurrence is the inscription "Know Thyself" at the oracle at Delphi. Thomas's statement "the Kingdom is within you and outside of you" places that Gospel in the context of ancient philosophical speculation and affirms the goodness of both human nature and of the nature of the outside world in an unambiguous fashion. Being Sons of the Father is to be like Jesus himself, a status one does not attain anew but that one realizes one has always had. Accordingly, self-discovery is the key to finding the potential wealth buried in people and in the world.

3a Jesus said: If your leaders say to you "Look! The Kingdom is in the sky!" Then the birds will be there before you are. If they say that the Kingdom is in the sea, then the fish will be there before you are. Rather, the Kingdom is within you and it is outside of you.[4]

3b When you understand yourselves you will be understood. And you will realize that you are Sons of the living Father. If you do not know yourselves, then you exist in poverty and you are that poverty.[5]

6 The specific symbolism of a "seven-day-old" infant suggests a time before circumcision, which was performed on the eighth day (and according to Thomas, circumcision is a senseless custom [saying 53]). The infant of seven days may also refer to the Image of God, who existed on the seventh day before the second round of creation brought Adam into being. The old man probably represents the ordinary person who has not sought or found the Kingdom. The infant as a model for wisdom can be found in other sayings in this Gospel as well, signifying that people must find a way to return to the beginning of their world and the time of the first creation. Saying 4 implies that the experience of discovery is no respecter of persons. The social categories of youth and age, and being socially first or last—these are irrelevant matters.

7 If what is hidden is the Kingdom, as saying 3 seems to indicate, its location is here in the present world. The Kingdom is everywhere now. In their separate ways, sayings 5 and 3 both deny that one's quest should lead one away from one's present circumstances. This contrasts strikingly with the more familiar early Christian opinion that the Kingdom is an event to be anticipated in the future or that the Kingdom is presently somewhere other than here. It also contrasts with the tendency of mystical speculations to create a complex system of truths that are difficult to comprehend. Thomas declares that it is all very obvious and easy to comprehend, once one has found the key to seeing things in the new way Jesus recommends.

4a Jesus said: The old man will not hesitate to ask a seven-day-old baby about the place of life, and he will live.[6]

4b For there are many who are first who will become last. They will become a single one.

5 Jesus said: Recognize what is right in front of you, and that which is hidden from you will be revealed to you. Nothing hidden will fail to be displayed.[7]

8 One of the puzzles of the Thomas document is the fact that the straightforward answers to the questions posed here appear in saying 14a. The answers given here are much more indirect. Nevertheless, they fit well with the principle introduced previously that what is hidden will be revealed. The indirect answers to questions about religious practices indicate that finding what is hidden takes precedence over concerns about prayer and fasting and charitable donations. "Do not do what you hate" is a version of the golden rule: "Do to others what you would have them do to you" because if it is spelled out it will be "Do not do to others what you hate to have done to yourself."

9 This saying seems to demand a kind of structure that it lacks because it seems to demand that its conclusion be phrased "because that man will become a lion," but it has a different conclusion. The first clause has to do with the process of simple digestion; a human who eats a lion incorporates that meat into a human body. Metaphorically it speaks of people turning ignorance and evil into good. The second clause speaks of ignorance and evil taking over a human being and turning a human into something less than human.

10 Saying 8 focuses on the act of finding. The discovery of the great fish is accidental; it is part of an ordinary catch drawn from the sea in the ordinary way, but the wisdom of the fisherman is to recognize and to choose the finest part. The great fish is, therefore, a symbol of something already out there in the world whose discovery can occur in the ordinary course of events. Realizing the value of what has been found is the real accomplishment.

6 His disciples questioned him: Should we fast? In what way should we pray? Should we give to charity? From which foods should we abstain? Jesus responded: Do not lie. If there is something that you hate, do not do it, for everything is revealed beneath heaven. Nothing hidden will fail to be displayed. Nothing covered will remain undisclosed.[8]

7 Jesus said: Blessed is a lion that a man eats, because that lion will become human. Cursed is a man that a lion eats, because that lion will become human.[9]

8 And he said: The man is like a thoughtful fisherman who threw his net into the sea and pulled it out full of little fish. Among all the little fish, that thoughtful fisherman found one fine large fish that would be beneficial to him and, throwing all the little fish back into the sea, he easily chose to keep the large one. Whoever has ears to hear let him hear.[10]

11 The oddest feature of the parable of the sower is the utter incompetence of the sower, for, as any gardener or farmer knows, seed is valuable and is not to be flung randomly about onto roads and stones and weedy places. Like the preceding parable of the fisherman, the parable of the sower seems to point to an element of randomness, for just as the excellent fish is found by chance, so the fact that some seed successfully grows is due to chance. The sower does not care where the seed falls; it is only by chance that any grows at all. But grow it does. The parable emphasizes the potential already existing in the world to produce results; it does not emphasize the special power of the sower. The notion of the seed being sown everywhere implies the presence of the Kingdom everywhere. But even if it is present everywhere, it may not be recognized everywhere or by everyone.

12 In the context of the Gospel of Thomas, the blazing of the fire that Jesus has cast will fall on individuals fanning that fire, cast in the past, into a blaze for themselves. The fire will not be some world-historical event that will take place in the indefinite future; it is not some coming day of judgment. Here the fire may represent Jesus' words, for it is the sayings of Jesus that Thomas's Gospel values most. In saying 82, Jesus says, "Whoever is near to me is near the fire. Whoever is far from me is far from the Kingdom" in a manner that equates the terms "fire" and "Kingdom." Here, when he throws fire upon the world we probably should understand that he has come to reveal knowledge of the Kingdom that is spread out upon the world.

9 Jesus said: Look, there was a man who came out to sow seed. He filled his hand with seed and threw it about. Some fell onto the road, and birds ate it. Some fell onto rocks and could not root and produced no grain. Some fell into patches of thorny weeds that kept it from growing, and grubs ate it. Some seed fell upon good soil and grew and produced good grain. It was 60 units per measure and 120 units per measure.[11]

10 Jesus said: I have thrown fire on the world. Look! I watch it until it blazes.[12]

13 Here Jesus highlights the fact that living people depend on eating dead plants and animals. They take dead things and, through digestion, incorporate them into themselves and make them alive. Jesus' statement in saying 7 also has this process in mind, for thereby a lion, eaten, becomes human. The implicit answer to the question "what will you do when you arrive into light?" is "eat living things"; in saying 111 we hear that "Anyone living from the living will not die." Such sayings support a vegetarian criticism of meat-eating, because eating "dead things" or animal flesh seems to be a practice that is ended when one begins to live from the living.

14 The final section of this saying may refer all the way back to the beginning of the human race. In mythic time the first person, Adam, became two people, Adam and Eve—a division that ultimately led to their fall. The restoration of the condition of human perfection is, symbolically, the restoration of unity between two so that they become "a single one." Those who find the Kingdom should, accordingly, be single ones.

15 James is Jesus' brother. Mark lists four brothers by name—James, Joses, Judas, Simon—and tells us that Jesus had sisters as well (Mark 6:3). After Jesus' death his brother became leader of the movement he founded, for Paul refers to "James, brother of the Lord" exercising authority even over Peter (Galatians 2:11–12). James became famous in the Christian movement for his righteousness, and the nickname "the Just" was applied to him. The present saying presumes that Jesus will be gone and need replacement as leader of the movement. Accordingly, Thomas advocates allegiance not to "the risen Lord" but to a human successor, James, who is commended for his own righteousness and not just because Jesus chose him.

11a Jesus said: This sky will cease to be, and the sky above it will cease to be.

11b The dead do not live, and the living will not die.

11c When you ate dead things, you made them alive. When you arrive into light, what will you do?[13]

11d When you were one, you became two. When you become two, what will you do?[14]

12 His disciples said to Jesus: We know you will leave us. Who will be our leader then? Jesus responded: Wherever you are, turn to Jacob [James] the Just, for whose sake the sky and the earth came into being.[15]

16 This saying is the only one that mentions Thomas at all, so it is probably the reason why the text was given the name and introductory comment that it now has. What Jesus is cannot be put into words. Because Thomas realizes this, he receives Jesus' highest approval.

17 Jesus' statement to Thomas, "I am not your teacher; you have drunk from and become intoxicated from the bubbling water that I poured out," brings to mind saying 108, which also refers to drinking from Jesus. These references may reveal an underlying metaphor: that Jesus' words are a fountain of wisdom. Even more than that, they show that Jesus and Thomas are no longer in a superior-inferior relationship but that they have become equivalent to each other. Both are, presumably, Sons of the living Father, as saying 3 reveals.

18 We do not know what the mysterious "three sayings" or "three words" are that Jesus spoke to Thomas, but clearly they were utterances that would result in violent reaction, even from Jesus' own followers. They would have sounded blasphemous, for throwing stones was a prescribed punishment for blasphemy. Perhaps the "fire" Jesus is said to have thrown upon the world (saying 10) is the fire that would come out of the stones cast at Thomas.

13 Jesus asked his disciples: Make a comparison; what am I like? Simon Peter replied: You are like a righteous messenger. Matthew replied: You are like an intelligent lover of wisdom. Thomas replied: Teacher, I cannot possibly say what you are like.[16] Jesus said to Thomas: I am not your teacher; you have drunk from and become intoxicated from the bubbling water that I poured out.[17] Jesus took Thomas and they withdrew. Jesus said three things to him. When Thomas returned to the other disciples, they asked him: What did Jesus tell you? Thomas replied: If I tell you even one of the sayings that he told me, you would pick up stones and throw them at me, and fire would come out of those stones and burn you up.[18]

19 These are the direct answers to the questions Jesus' disciples asked him in saying 6. The first three directives in saying 14a appear in no other Christian texts for reasons that should be obvious: they contradict central Christian teachings. Saying 14a follows directly after saying 13 because Thomas's author believed that these three statements were the secret "three sayings" given in saying 13. They do border on blasphemy, and they would have shocked most Christians or Jews who heard them.

The prohibitions of fasting, prayer, and giving in charity are logical, from Thomas's perspective. If one's principal religious duty is to seek and find the hidden Kingdom, when you succeed and return successfully to the condition of the Beginning, turning to God in prayer or repentance is irrelevant or misguided. You exist in a mythical time before sin came into being.

Thomas consistently expresses confidence in the human ability to discover hidden truth without any direct divine help or intervention. If you rely on divine help through prayer, or on repentance through fasting, or on obedience through acts of charity, you are going in the wrong direction.

20 Saying 14b is the only reference to healing in the Gospel of Thomas, but the main point of the saying and the reason it is included at this place in the Gospel is the command "eat whatever they provide for you," because it answers the question raised by the food taboos of formal Jewish religion, which is this: Are those taboos binding on Christians, or not? Any Christian who eats ham or shrimp knows the taboos were canceled. Jesus' disciples are told to eat whatever they are given, to ignore taboos.

21 Mark tells us that by means of this saying Jesus suspended the Hebrew scripture laws regarding food: "Thus he declared all foods clean" (Mark 7:19b). People reading Thomas are sometimes surprised to discover that Jesus spoke against common religious practices. According to Mark, people were once surprised to find him doing so, too.

14a Jesus said to them: If you fast you will bring sin to yourselves, and if you pray you will be condemned, and if you give to charity you will damage your spirits.[19]

14b When you go into a region and walk around in the rural areas, whenever people receive you, eat whatever they provide for you, and heal their sick.[20]

14c For what goes into your mouth
will not defile you, but what comes out of your mouth can defile you.[21]

22 Matthew and Luke portray Jesus saying, about John the Baptist, that "*among those born of women* there has risen no one greater than John the Baptist: yet he who is least in the Kingdom of Heaven is greater than he." Implicitly there are two categories of people: those who are born from a woman and those who are not. The people who are not born from a woman are in the Kingdom of Heaven. However great John the Baptist may be, they are greater than he, because they are in the Kingdom and he, by implication, is not.

Saying 15 could be speaking of those who are "born again": people who are therefore not born from a woman. Rebirth in the context of the Gospel of Thomas involves a revolution of perceptions about oneself and the world, the discovery in the world of the presence of the Kingdom. It includes the rediscovery of the Beginning, when the Image of God was born but was *not* born from a woman.

❖ "If one examines all the surviving sayings attributed to Jesus, no matter where, a wide range of religious perspectives can be found: wisdom sayings and proverbs reminiscent of Old Testament wisdom books; prophetic sayings pronouncing God's judgment; eschatological sayings; legal sayings regulating community life; Christological sayings, in which Jesus describes or predicts his role and position. Against this background it is obvious that [the Gospel of Thomas] is by no means a well-distributed sample of these usual saying types, but rather concentrates on particular types that are appropriate to its message of salvation—especially wisdom sayings or general truths, and prophetic sayings that emphasize the presence of God's reign ('kingdom') within Jesus and each believer."

—Bentley Layton, *The Gnostic Scriptures*, pp. 376–377

15 Jesus said: When you see someone not born from a woman, prostrate yourselves and worship him; he is your Father.[22]

23 Ironically, the vast majority of Christians—in the United States at least—seem to think of Jesus *primarily* as one who came to throw peace upon the world and to bring loving harmony to families. Evidently Jesus disagreed with that assessment. People whose notion of Jesus focuses on his status as "Prince of Peace" seem to be relying exclusively on a phrase found in Isaiah 9:7 but found nowhere in the New Testament.

The final statement "And they will stand up and they will be *alone*" uses the term *monachos*, the Greek word for people who are single or alone; the English word "monk" derives from *monachos*. In Thomas, the word characterizes those who opt out of worldly life to live in the direct presence of the Kingdom of Heaven.

❖ "A number of scholars have developed summaries of this Gospel's theology, but ultimately no summary will be able to capture the interactive and intellectually challenging process of hearing the sayings pronounced by Jesus and finding their interpretation. This attentive reading is, after all, the suggested strategy presented by the Gospel itself."

—Richard Valantasis, *The Gospel of Thomas*, p. 12

16a Jesus said: People think, perhaps, that I have come to throw peace upon the world. They don't know that I have come to throw disagreement upon the world, and fire, and sword, and struggle.

16b [For] there will be five in one house. Three will oppose two. Two will oppose three. The father will oppose his son and the son oppose his father. And they will stand up and they will be alone [*monachos*].[23]

24 A statement quite similar to Thomas 17 occurs in Paul's First Letter to the Corinthians (1 Corinthians 2:7–10) where Paul refers to this saying in the context of "God's wisdom secret and hidden, which God decreed before the ages" and refers to it as "what is written," as if it had been quoted from scripture, but no Hebrew scripture passage is the same. The First Letter of John begins: "We declare to you what was from the beginning, what we have heard, what we have seen with our eyes, what we have looked at and touched with our hands, concerning the word of life—this life was revealed, and we have seen it and testify to it." According to John's letter, what was hidden from the beginning has already been revealed: Jesus the incarnate word. Saying 17 in Thomas is followed by two sayings, 18 and 19, referring to the primordial past. Paul, Thomas, and John are all thinking of Jesus' hidden things in terms of primordial time.

Saying 17 reveals that Jesus gives something never previously experienced. While one would normally expect to hear what sort of thing it is that Jesus gives, details are not supplied. We can observe, however, that it is not completely in the realm of ideas. It can be touched. It can be heard and seen as well as thought. In Thomas 3a, the Kingdom is said to be located within *and outside* of people. The Kingdom within is a Thomasine theme, to be sure, but it should not overwhelm the theme of the Kingdom as outside, visible, audible, tangible.

17 Jesus said: I will give you that which eyes have not seen, ears have not heard, hands did not touch, and minds have not conceived.[24]

25 The Gospel of Thomas often portrays the disciples as ignorant of Jesus' fundamental message. As usual, here they act as foils, asking the wrong question from the wrong perspective in order to provide Jesus a chance to correct them. Their question shows that they expect a future Kingdom—an expectation that has characterized orthodox Christians for two thousand years. Here Jesus rejects that form of Christianity. He insists on a reorientation toward the Beginning of time. The Beginning is the first days of creation as described in Genesis 1–4. That is a special kind of time, time that is always present-time, even though it is not always perceived. You can find it right in front of you now. If you do not find it, it does not exist for you except in potential, and you remain in poverty even though you are surrounded by riches.

Saying 18b is a beatitude, affirming the blessing of all who have found the Beginning now and, simultaneously, who have experienced the end, for the ending is a return to the Beginning. Such people have discovered their original form, the Image of God, and the Image of God can never die.

❖ "Whereas Q emphasized the eschatological expectation of the future coming of the 'Kingdom of God,' the Gospel of Thomas in its oldest form stressed the finding of wisdom, or of the 'Kingdom of the Father,' in the knowledge *(gnosis)* of oneself (cf. saying 3), guided by the sayings of Jesus. This understanding of salvation is similar to that expressed in many passages of the Gospel of John in which the finding of truth and life is bound to the words of Jesus (John 6:63; 851)."

—Helmut Koester, "Introduction," in *The Nag Hammadi Library in English*, p. 125

18a The disciples asked Jesus: Tell us about our end. What will it be? Jesus replied: Have you found the Beginning so that you now seek the end? The place of the Beginning will be the place of the end.

18b Blessed is anyone who will stand up in the Beginning and thereby know the end and never die.[25]

26 Thomas's sayings sometimes are based on the fact that there are two creation stories in Genesis. The first begins at Genesis 1:1 and ends at 2:3. The second begins at 2:4 and continues indefinitely. The first creation is perfect. God declares it "good" seven separate times. The first creation features the origin of light and of the primordial humanity made in the Image of God. The second creation starts as if the first had never taken place and features the creation of man out of dirt and the creation of woman out of the man's rib.

Ancient (and present-day) readers sometimes wondered what happened to the first creation. Such a good creation would not just disappear for no reason. Since the first is never said to have ceased to be, then it must coexist along with the second in a condition of perfection unmarred by any fall subsequent to the primordial seventh day.

From Thomas's perspective, the ultimate goal for human beings is to enter into the condition of the first creation—a condition that continues to exist in reality, although the second creation is what virtually everyone ordinarily perceives. Thomas calls the first hidden creation "the Kingdom of Heaven." The human condition of any person can be that of the original Image of God or that of the Adam from the second creation. Accordingly, those who exist before coming into being are humans in the manner of the Image of God, which existed (Genesis 1:26–27) before humans in the form of Adam came into being (Genesis 2:7). Both continue simultaneously to exist, but the later and inferior form masks the former primordial form.

27 Since the Kingdom of Heaven is here now upon the earth, everything on earth will serve disciples who recognize that fact. We hear in the Genesis story of the first creation that humans will have dominion over all things on earth (Genesis 1:28–30). The very stones serve those who recognize their own true nature and the true nature of the world.

The five trees of paradise may allude to the rivers of the four directions, specified in Genesis 2:11–14 along with the center, Eden, from which the rivers flow (Genesis 2:10). These rivers water the trees of paradise (Genesis 2:9). To come to know the trees of paradise, one must return to the condition of the Beginning.

19a Jesus said: Blessed is one who existed before coming into being.[26]

19b If you become my disciples and listen to me, these stones will serve you.

19c In paradise there are five trees that do not change between summer and winter, and their leaves never fall. Anyone who comes to know them will not die.[27]

28 Mustard is a weed, not a crop; it is a colonizing plant that quickly takes over newly broken ground. Thomas's description is botanically correct; the seeds of mustard fall onto worked or plowed or open ground and mustard plants rise up without any human effort involved. Just as a large fish is found in a net full of small fish, or some randomly sown seed grows successfully, mustard seed falls accidentally on suitable ground and flourishes. The mustard seed can be said to be symbolic of "faith," or of "the church," or of "the Kingdom of Heaven." These are not demonstrably false allegorical guesses, but they are not explanations that are present in the original. In seeking the meaning of Jesus' sayings in Thomas, one should not automatically assume the correctness of church-based or even evangelist-based speculations about their meanings.

20 The disciples said to Jesus: Tell us what the Kingdom of Heaven is like. He replied: It is like a mustard seed, the smallest of all. However, when it falls into worked ground it sends out a large stem, and it becomes a shelter for the birds of heaven.[28]

29 We know of Mary, the mother of Jesus, Mary Magdalene, Mary the mother of James and Joses, and Mary the mother of John Mark from the New Testament, but which "Mary" is addressing Jesus here we have no way of knowing. Since Jesus' disciples, as they are presented in the Gospel of Thomas, rarely seem to have any clear idea of what Jesus is trying to communicate, and therefore repeatedly ask misguided questions, one should not automatically assume that "what are your disciples like?" is the equivalent of "what are those who correctly understand like?" It could be the opposite. The disciples may represent illegitimate claimants to Christian understanding, and the field they stand in may possibly be the church as Thomas understands it.

30 The motif of stripping naked refers to the ideal primordial time before the fall, prior to which Adam and Eve were naked and unashamed (Genesis 2:25). Subsequently they became aware of their nakedness and were ashamed (Genesis 3:7). The Gospel of Thomas advocates return to the time of the Beginning, and so also to the nakedness symbolic of that time.

31 In Thomas's Gospel, people are capable of finding treasure and discovering the Kingdom, yet they are also capable of losing what they have found. The "world" here represents what are commonly called "worldly things." It is certainly not that world upon which the Kingdom of Heaven is spread. Nothing in Thomas argues that the whole "material world" itself is to be contrasted with the "spiritual world."

21a Mary asked Jesus: Who are your disciples like?[29]
He replied: They are like little children in a field
that does not belong to them. When the field's
owners come they will say: "Give our field back."
They will strip naked in the owners' presence and
give it back, returning their field to them.[30]

21b Therefore I say: If a householder knows a thief
is coming, he will keep watch and not let him break
into his house (of his kingdom) and steal his goods.

21c You must keep watch against the world,
preparing yourselves with power so that thieves
will not find any way to come upon you.[31]

21d The situation you are expecting will come.
Let a person who understands be with you.

21e After the grain had ripened, he quickly came,
carrying his sickle, and he harvested it.

21f He who has ears to hear, let him hear.

32 Saying 22 is one of the most striking of all those in the Gospel of Thomas. In saying 4 we hear of an infant of seven days being wiser than an old man. Here, too, the infants are very young. Many people imagine Jesus speaking of little children and imagine that these are children of at least toddler age, but when Jesus likens people eligible for the Kingdom to infants in the Gospel of Thomas, the infants are much younger than that. Ironically, of course, they are also extremely old; they are infants in respect to the foundation of the world, for their seven-day-old status probably relates to the seventh day of the original creation described in Genesis 1. They have returned to the Beginning.

33 In Genesis 1 we hear that the Image of God is made male and female. Genesis 1:27: "God created man in his image. In God's image he created him. Male and female he created them." Does this mean that God made the ideal person male in his own male image, or does it mean that God made the ideal person in his image and made that one being male and female? Surely it is the latter. There aren't two Gods making separate sexual images of themselves, after all. There is one God making one image, and since that image is made male and female, the primordial person is of both sexes. Accordingly, if the one who enters the Kingdom is to return to the seventh-day state of infancy, he will do so before the mythic time of the separation of the sexes (Genesis 2:22).

Since the main thrust of saying 22 has to do with male and female losing their distinctive characteristics, so that the male is not male nor the female female, it doesn't seem inappropriate to speculate that "make the inside like the outside and the outside like the inside" may refer to sexual organs, and that "the upper like the lower and the lower like the upper" may refer to positions of sexual intercourse.

The image of God is essentially one, male and female, perfect, immortal, ever present, and yet it is human. Therefore, the image of God has hands and eyes and feet and so forth. To find it is to find oneself and to be reborn back into the seventh day of creation. Then one enters the Kingdom.

22a Jesus saw infants being suckled. He said to his disciples: These infants taking milk are like those who enter the Kingdom.[32]

22b His disciples asked him: If we are infants will we enter the Kingdom? Jesus responded: When you make the two into one, and when you make the inside like the outside and the outside like the inside, and the upper like the lower and the lower like the upper, and thus make the male and the female the same, so that the male isn't male and the female isn't female. When you make an eye to replace an eye, and a hand to replace a hand, and a foot to replace a foot, and an image to replace an image, then you will enter the Kingdom.[33]

34 The transformation in perceptions that Thomas's sayings encourage is a very difficult one, and very few people are able to accomplish it. The "seek and find" ideology of Thomas is quite different than the "gift" ideology of the orthodox doctrine of grace. Thomas's sayings encourage individuals to find the Kingdom for themselves, within and outside themselves. Being one of those who are "chosen" therefore gives one the *opportunity* to quest for the Kingdom. It cannot be the case that some few people are "chosen" to receive the Kingdom as a gift.

35 The disciples again take the wrong approach. Their question, which appears to be nonsense, presupposes the orthodox view of Christianity: that Jesus Himself is the be-all and end-all of the Christian faith. Accordingly, finding the place where Jesus is, is what any Christian should do. Rather than find all the world, the orthodox view expressed here in the disciples' question is that finding the one place Jesus is will suffice. Jesus' response encourages breadth of inquiry. Just as saying 3 located the Kingdom within and outside of people, so this saying locates light inside and outside. Individuals' efforts are required. The man of light can illuminate the world or not. The saying assumes the logical possibility that a man of light can be darkness, and therefore his illumination of the world is not automatic and innate.

In order to see the world as the Kingdom of God, one must illuminate the world in a Kingdom-like manner. Therefore, self-transformation must come first. One restores oneself as the Image of God, as saying 22 urges, and at the Beginning, as saying 18 requires. Then one can illuminate the world outside as God's Kingdom in accordance with saying 24. One will then radiate out from within oneself the light of creation's first day, the supernal light that came before the creation of sun and stars.

23 Jesus said: I will choose one of you out of a thousand and two of you out of ten thousand. They will stand up and they will be alone.[34]

24 His disciples said to him: Show us the place you are, for it is essential for us to seek it. He responded: He who has ears let him hear. There is light within a man of light, and he lights up all of the world. If he is not alight there is darkness.[35]

36 The first record of the admonition to "love your neighbor as yourself" occurs in Leviticus 19:18. There its context is negative, focusing on what one should not do: "You should not take vengeance or bear a grudge against any of your people but you should love your neighbor as yourself." Here in the Gospel of Thomas the context is positive: "protect him."

37 This saying concludes with a proverb, common sense expressed cleverly with meaning that shifts depending on the context within which it is spoken. In the present context of saying 24, it admonishes a person of light to begin to shine forth radiance into the world before setting out to show others the way to do so. In the context of saying 25, one can understand it to urge people to prepare to protect their brothers by first making sure that they are strong enough to do so.

❖ "As a gospel of wisdom, the Gospel of Thomas proclaims a distinctive message. In contrast to the way in which he is portrayed in other gospels, particularly New Testament gospels, Jesus in the Gospel of Thomas performs no physical miracles, reveals no fulfillment of prophecy, announces no apocalyptic kingdom about to disrupt the world order, and dies for no one's sins. Instead, Thomas's Jesus dispenses insight from the bubbling spring of wisdom (saying 13), discounts the value of prophecy and its fulfillment (saying 52), critiques end-of-the-world, apocalyptic announcements (sayings 51, 113), and offers a way of salvation through an encounter with the sayings of 'the living Jesus.'"

—Marvin Meyer, *The Hidden Sayings of Jesus*, p. 10

25 Jesus said: Love your brother as your own soul. Protect him as you protect the pupil of your eye.[36]

26 Jesus said: You see the splinter in your brother's eye, but you do not see the log that is in your own eye. Remove the log from your own eye, and then you can clearly see to remove the splinter from your brother's eye.[37]

38 Since the Kingdom of Heaven is already available on the earth within and outside people, they should become able to see it through their own inner light. What then of the former world, the world of fallenness and of religious obligations and prayer and repentance and so forth? That world needs to be put aside. Instead, one should radiate light into the world and receive that light back from the Kingdom. Accordingly, the less one interacts with the common perspectives of the world, the more one may come to see it in the new light of the Kingdom of Heaven. Thus, one should fast from the world as it ordinarily is in order to find the world to be the Kingdom of Heaven.

39 The practice of keeping the Sabbath is also a form of fasting, for to keep the Sabbath one refrains from work, just as one refrains from food in order to fast. It seems unlikely that Thomas's Gospel affirms the necessity of keeping standard Jewish religious conventions here, but speaks out against them in saying 14. Rather, the Thomasine community probably understood the Sabbath as a transformed way of interacting with the world, just as it understood fasting that way. So as one fasts from the world, so also one "Sabbaths" from the world.

Thomas probably has in mind the Sabbath of the Beginning, the Sabbath of the seventh day (Genesis 2:1–3), when God rested and blessed the seventh day and hallowed it. In accordance with the mythological thinking Thomas employs, after the Fall the first creation did not cease to exist, but it did become difficult to recognize. It must be sought and found. The Sabbath of the seventh day did not cease; it is the continuing state of the world-as-Kingdom, and perfected seven-day-old children dwell in that Sabbath. To find this state and live in it is the goal of the Gospel of Thomas.

27a If you do not fast from the world you will not find the Kingdom.[38]

27b If you do not keep the Sabbath as a Sabbath you will never see the Father.[39]

40 In the Hebrew scripture Book of Proverbs, God's Wisdom is sometimes presented as a semi-independent aspect of God, a feminine presence who comes into the world offering people access to her wisdom, which, if they take it in, guarantees them successful lives. Sometimes people respond positively, but often Wisdom laments her inability to communicate with anyone at all. "Wisdom cries out in the street; in the squares she raises her voice. At the busiest corner she cries out; at the entrance of the city she speaks…'I have called and you refused, have stretched out my hand and no one heeded'" (Proverbs 1:21–24). In saying 28 of the Gospel of Thomas, Jesus speaks as Wisdom. He has come into the world but finds no one willing to fill himself or herself with what he offers. People arrive in the world empty and go out empty. Empty of what? In this context the answer should be "empty of wisdom."

When Jesus says "I came to them in the flesh" here in saying 28, it is a potent statement within a powerful first-century controversy. Some Christians claimed that Jesus was only Spirit, others that he had human flesh. In this saying, for a change, Thomas's gospel takes the orthodox position on an issue.

❖ "An element that sets the Gospel of Thomas most sharply apart from the Jesus-sayings in the canon is the repeated message that one's goal should be a reuniting of opposites, an end to the differentness of things that is a mark of this world, a grasping of oneness—in short, the experience of unity."

—Herbert Christian Merillat, *The Gnostic Apostle Thomas*, p. 184

28 Jesus said: I stood in the midst of the world. I came to them in the flesh *[sarx]*. I found all of them drunk. I found not one of them to be thirsty. My soul was saddened by the sons of men for they are mentally blind. They do not see that they have come into the world empty and they will go out of the world empty. But now they are drunk. When they sober up they will repent.[40]

41 A mythic theory of the origin of things is implied here. Two propositions are suggested:

1. Flesh *(sarx)* came into being because of spirit *(pneuma)*.
2. Spirit *(pneuma)* came into being because of body *(soma)*.

If we understand body and flesh to be the same thing (and it is hard to imagine any reason to do otherwise), then propositions 1 and 2 are opposites. Either one is true or the other is true, but both simultaneously cannot be true. The question then might be, which of the two is Jesus affirming? The answer must be that he affirms the second one, because, while the first is said to describe a state of affairs that would be "wonderful," the second describes something "exceedingly wonderful" and so it takes precedence. Accordingly, in a roundabout manner, saying 29b appears to have Jesus affirm the proposition "The spirit came into being because of the body." This proposition is not particularly surprising, for it may restate the mythic theme of the precedence of body over spirit that is found in Genesis 2:7, where first the body comes into being from clay, through God's creative power, and then subsequently God breathes into, or "inspirits," the clay with life. The inspirited clay begins life, though, in the world of "poverty" (saying 3), ignorant of the wealth of the Kingdom that lies awaiting discovery.

42 Perhaps saying 30 is a slap against Trinitarian doctrine, asserting that a doctrine of three Gods is polytheistic if one understands that each of the Gods is a separate God. The saying may go on to assert that where there is one (God) alone with a person, then Jesus is with him too and so two are with him.

29 Jesus said: If flesh *[sarx]* came into being because of spirit, it is wonderful. If spirit came into being because of the body, it is exceedingly wonderful. I am amazed that this great wealth has appeared in this poverty.[41]

30 Jesus said: Where there are three Gods they are Gods. Where there are two or one, I am with him.[42]

43 If you have a special relationship with the supernatural, you are going to have a much greater chance of convincing others of that fact if you are somewhere away from home rather than where you grew up. That common sense applies to Jesus, who was a prophet and a healer. Such people would be more successful among strangers, and this proverb attests to that fact.

The author of the Gospel of Mark created a life of Jesus from the sources available to him, few of which were narratives. One of Mark's principal sources was the sayings of Jesus, which he may have taken from some written texts as well as from oral tradition. Mark set out to construct a biography partially from isolated decontextualized sayings. We can follow him doing so as he creates his Gospel's chapter 6:1–6 from this proverb, writing of Jesus' return to his home town, their rejection of him as a prophet, his failure to heal those who knew him, and then concluding with Jesus speaking a version of this very saying.

44 This saying urges strength in defense while at the same time encouraging openness. You should not try to protect yourself by hiding your light, but at the same time you should be aware that attacks are likely. Ultimately you will be safe, above real danger, even if you expose yourself and your light to the world.

45 The first part of this saying shows that the Thomas sayings were not to be kept secret but transmitted widely. They are sometimes called secret sayings, but that is because their meanings are obscure and hard to figure out. The sayings themselves are public and should be preached from housetops. Saying 33b became a proverb in English-speaking lands, for everyone knows that "you shouldn't hide your light under a bushel."

31 Jesus said: No prophet is accepted in his own village. No physician heals the people who know him well.[43]

32 Jesus said: A city built and fortified atop a tall hill cannot be taken, nor can it be hidden.[44]

33a Jesus said: What you hear in your ears preach from your housetops.

33b For nobody lights a lamp and puts it underneath a bushel basket or in a hidden place. Rather, it is placed on a lamp stand so that all who go in and out may see the light.[45]

46 Like others before him who probably used this proverb, and like those after him who certainly used it, Jesus gave this proverb significance when he used it in a particular conversation to make a point within a specific context. In Thomas we have no conversational context for the proverb at all; such a context can only occur in a narrative gospel. One principal motivation for writing the narrative gospels was probably the authors' desire to make Jesus' sayings meaningful through the creation of contexts for them.

If "blindness" refers to spiritual blindness here, then the saying may be a dig against religious leaders who have no clue. Saying 3 sarcastically criticizes such people. In saying 28, Jesus complains about the spiritual blindness of people in general, and the parable of saying 34 may also criticize spiritual blindness.

47 This statement is clear and commonsense, accordingly it is a proverb. We have no idea what context it originally had in the life of Jesus, although Mark (3:27) has Jesus use the "strong man" as an allegory for Satan. If so, then the saying has to do with the necessity to first exorcise and bind demons before trying to overcome their influence in the world.

48 Like other sayings in Thomas, this one criticizes people's overinvolvement in the ordinary social world. Similarly, saying 78 contrasts Jesus himself, in the desert, with royal courtiers who are magnificently dressed but who will not know the truth.

34 Jesus said: If a blind person leads another blind person, both of them will fall into a ditch.[46]

35 Jesus said: It is not possible for anyone to enter a strong man's house and take it over forcefully unless he first ties his hands. Then he can steal from that house.[47]

36 Jesus said: Do not worry from morning to evening or evening to morning about what you are going to wear.[48]

49 This saying arises from the idea that the attainment of perfection is a return to the beginning. One should retrace one's steps as a human being back through mythical time to the period before the Fall. Then one will be naked and unashamed, a little child at the Beginning of time. Adam and Eve's symbolic shame at discovering their own nakedness, and their subsequent donning of clothing, is to be ritually reversed, according to Jesus.

Unless it is assumed that Jesus will come back in the future in a transformed mode, the question "When will we see you?" is trivially absurd. The disciples once again are representative of orthodox eschatological Christianity, for their question supposes that the crucial factors regarding the Christian religion are going to happen in the future in a public manner. In that glorious future, Jesus will appear in his second coming, and they will be able to see Jesus as he truly is. But to focus on Jesus' own person, rather than on the light of the Kingdom within the world, is misguided.

From the perspective of the Gospel of Thomas, the questions and their implications are completely misguided because the disciples' focus should not be on Jesus personally as the agent of salvation but on themselves as capable of individual transformation. Accordingly, a question about Jesus is answered by reference to the transformation of the questioner. Furthermore, the presupposition of the questions—that the crucial events of the future are what matter—is reoriented by Jesus' answer, which points back to the immediate present status of the questioner. There will be no public event of salvation to come and change the world. Rather, the questioners will succeed when they themselves are changed. Saying 3 promises, "you will realize that you are Sons of the living Father," and here, saying 37 contains enigmatic advice as to how to achieve that realization. Looking outside yourself to find where Jesus himself is, or awaiting his arrival, is not the right approach.

37 His disciples asked him: When will you appear to us? When will we see you? Jesus replied: When you strip naked without shame and trample your clothing underfoot just as little children do, then you will look at the son of the living one without being afraid.[49]

50 Jesus' disciples have failed to understand him. Accordingly, although they could hear Jesus speaking while they were with him, they nevertheless will start to seek him in the proper manner only when it is too late. This is in accord with the Gospel of Thomas's view that the disciples were people who inspired the mistaken future-oriented and Jesus-focused Christianity that came to be dominant in the orthodox Church. Such people do not understand that they must look to the present and to themselves. Thus, while his disciples have wanted to hear from Jesus, and know that his words are unique to him, they lose the unique opportunity given them because they have failed to understand. When they come to realize their mistake it will be too late.

The second sentence of saying 38 does not necessarily mean that disciples should seek Jesus. It may be spoken with irony: "you will seek me and you will not be able to find me" in the future. Seeking Jesus sounds like a fine idea from the orthodox perspective. But from the Thomasine viewpoint, people seek within themselves and in the world now, and in reference to the primordial Beginning, rather than looking outside themselves for Jesus.

❖ "Nothing mediates the self for the Jesus of the Gospel of Thomas. Everything we seek is already in our presence, and not outside our self. What is most remarkable in these sayings is the repeated insistence that everything is already open to you. You need but knock and enter. What is best and oldest in you will respond fully to what you allow yourself to see."

—Harold Bloom, "A Reading," in *The Gospel of Thomas*, edited by Marvin Meyer, p. 112

38 Jesus said: You often wanted to hear the words
I am speaking to you. You have no one else
from whom you can hear them. The days will come
when you will seek me and you will not be able
to find me.[50]

51 The biblical gospels portray categories of Jewish leaders as dedicated enemies of Jesus: scribes, Pharisees, lawyers, priests, Herodians, Saducees. But with few exceptions, Jesus' implied adversaries in the Gospel of Thomas are Christians, most often signified by Jesus' misguided disciples. Saying 39 is an exception; there his adversaries are Pharisees and scribes. The only other Thomas saying that mentions scribes or Pharisees is Thomas 102. While it conveys the same general opinion of them as saying number 39 does, the wording is so different that we clearly have two separate sayings rather than two versions of one.

The saying in Thomas is typically obscure. It is assumed that the Pharisees and scribes do in fact have the keys of knowledge, whatever they might be, and that they have not taken advantage of their possession of those keys, and that they will let no one else take advantage either. The Pharisees and scribes were characterized by their knowledge of the Torah, the five Books of Moses that begin the Hebrew Bible. It is reasonable to assume that the saying refers to their skill at interpreting the Torah, for the simple reason that that was what they were most skilled at. The Pharisees claimed to have access to an "Oral Torah" in addition to the written books of Moses, and perhaps their knowledge of that special source of revelation about God's Law was the "key of knowledge" under discussion.

52 It is easiest to assume that the Father represents God, so if something is planted outside the Father, it would be guaranteed to fail because of the principle that divine sustenance is essential to life. In this saying, the grapevine does fail and is destroyed. There is no indication of who planted this grapevine, or why, nor do we know what the grapevine represents. We have no clue who "they" are who will pull it up; are "they" supernatural angels or natural human beings? If humans, what sort? We certainly cannot be sure what "outside of the Father" means. All one can really state is that the saying may express the ordinary wisdom of benevolent monotheism: that nothing thrives in the absence of God.

39a Jesus said: The Pharisees and the scribes have taken the keys to knowledge and have hidden them. They did not go in, and they did not permit those desiring to go in to enter.

39b You should be as clever as snakes and as innocent as doves.[51]

40 Jesus said: A grapevine was planted outside of the Father but, as it did not strengthen, they will pull it up by its roots and it will die.[52]

53 There is a proverb in the English language that has the same meaning as this one: "The rich get richer and the poor get poorer." At first glance, though, saying 41 seems enigmatic, for—as is usual in the Gospel of Thomas—the significance of the principal terms is unknown. Whoever possesses some of what? As is the case with any proverb, that question would have been answered within the context of the particular conversation whenever the proverb was applied.

Matthew makes an interesting application of this proverb when he has Jesus use it in reference to the mysteries of the Kingdom of Heaven (13:12). Some people may have a little access to "the mysteries," but if they fail to take advantage they will lose everything. Others, who are the seekers, find that more and more access opens to them over time.

54 Its very brevity has given this saying in Thomas a degree of fame. It can just as well be translated "be passers-by" or "be itinerant." As is usually the case in the Gospel of Thomas, a context is both demanded and missing. Jesus said this to whom? When? Under what circumstances? Of course, we do not know. When a saying attributed to Jesus is devoid of context, those readers who hold Jesus in high respect generally assume that in some sense or other the saying has relevance to them and their lives in their context. The evangelists, beginning with Mark, saw it as their duty to bring meaning to sayings by providing narrative biographical contexts for them, and thus a life of Jesus came into being. Thomas's Gospel gives us good examples of the kinds of raw material the evangelists used in their work.

In its original first-century context, it is possible that saying 42 encouraged people to "fast from the world" and not to become involved in what are called worldly affairs. Alternatively, it may have been said in order to require Christian itinerant missionaries to keep on the move, not to settle in one place, not even to stay in one house for more than a brief period, which would be in keeping with the instructions found in Luke's Gospel (9:57–10:12). One might interpret this shortest of sayings either as encouraging a lifestyle of missionary homelessness in a literal sense, or as encouraging dissatisfaction with worldly affairs in general and thus advocating homelessness in a metaphorical sense.

41 Jesus said: Whoever possesses some will be given more. Whoever possesses virtually nothing will have what little he does possess taken away.[53]

42 Jesus said: Be one of those who pass by.[54]

55 The Gospel of Thomas is a sayings list containing no stories of miracles, no virgin birth narrative, no discussion of Jesus' crucifixion, and no mention of a resurrection. As such, the document—and also possibly the people who compiled it—focuses attention exclusively on Jesus' sayings. To the Gospel of Thomas, Jesus' function is primarily if not exclusively to be a producer of words. In saying 43, the disciples—as always mistaken in their assumptions—try to discover what it is about Jesus that authorizes him to speak in such an authoritative manner. "Who are you," they ask, "to say these things?" What gives him the right? Who is the person behind the words? But seeking the person is a misguided approach; from Thomas's perspective, the words are what count. If Jesus has a special identity in the Thomasine context it is within the words, not as one who stands behind the words. Accordingly, he responds that he must be recognized from what he says as opposed to the disciples' implication that what he says must be validated by who he is.

In the ancient world the linguistic distinction we make in English between "Jew," for a person who belongs to a particular religion, and "Judean," for a person who derives from a particular region, was not made. The Greek word *Ioudaios* covered both categories and so, then, there was only one category. Jesus probably was not *Ioudaios*. He was, as everyone knows, a man from Nazareth in Galilee. Galilee and Judea were two different political and cultural places. Galilee had been separated from Judea for almost all of the seven hundred years prior to the birth of Jesus, conquered and controlled by a succession of rulers. Our naïve view of Galilee as part of a seamless whole with Judea is a product of present-day religious and political ideologies, and it is debatable to what extent an inhabitant of Galilee could be assumed to be sympathetic to the *Ioudaioi,* much less automatically assumed to be *Ioudaios*.

Saying 43 urges people not to be hypocritical, not divide what is a whole into two artificial categories and then side with one category against another. As a general rule, in the early Christian movement the metaphoric term "fruit" refers to human behaviors: "by their fruits

(continued on page 58)

43 His disciples asked him: Who are you
to say these things to us? Jesus replied:
Don't you recognize who I am from what I say to you?
You have become like the Jews who like the tree
but loathe its fruit, or they like the fruit but
loathe the tree.[55]

you will know them," and so forth. If that is the case with this saying, then Jesus seems to be criticizing Judeans for a tendency to separate an actor from his actions and then to side with one aspect or the other. Rather, a person and his actions should be thought of as an indissoluble unit. It is interesting to reflect on the fact that a Christian cliché of the present day, "love the sinner but hate the sin," seems to be exactly the sort of sentiment that is being criticized here.

56 The interpretation of saying 44 is a puzzle. Only in saying 44a does one hear about "the son." In saying 3, Christians are potentially "Sons of the living Father," and in saying 37, we hear that Christians may see "the son of the living one" in a context wherein one cannot be sure if this means the realization of their own potentials or if it means that they will see Jesus.

Thomas and Mark (3:28–30) differ as to whether blasphemy against the Holy Spirit will remain unforgiven in all places (Thomas: earth/heaven) or throughout all time (Mark: eternally). Thomas 44 may have been spoken by Jesus in reference to the fact that his particular power was thought to derive from the Holy Spirit, which he received at the time of his baptism by John. If his power to heal, to forgive sins, and to speak the word of God was thought to derive from the Holy Spirit, and if faith in his power was in some manner thought to be crucial, blasphemy against the Holy Spirit would absolutely contradict faith in Jesus. Thus, anyone blaspheming the Spirit would be entirely outside the Christian movement.

57 This saying is a simple proverb (45a) with a variety of applications (45b) added to it. As is often the case in the transmission of the sayings of Jesus, in this proverbial saying people added their comments about the meaning of the proverb onto the saying itself. Jesus certainly did use proverbs, and quite a few are quoted in his name. But we can be virtually certain that the explanations that they receive in our texts are from later Christians and not from Jesus himself.

44 Jesus said: Whoever blasphemes against the Father will be forgiven. Whoever blasphemes against the son will be forgiven. But whoever blasphemes against the Holy Spirit will not be forgiven, neither on earth nor in heaven.[56]

45a Jesus said: They do not pick grapes from brambles, nor do they pick figs from thistles, for these do not yield the proper fruit.

45b A good man brings good things out of his storehouse, but a bad man brings bad things from his storehouse (which is in his heart). And he says bad things. For out of the surplus in his heart he brings out bad things.[57]

58 Saying 46 repeats a claim made in saying 22. There Jesus says to his disciples: "These infants taking milk are like those who enter the Kingdom." Everyone in the Kingdom of God is greater than John, and everyone in the Kingdom is metaphorically an infant. Those who are infants in the Kingdom are self-born and so are not born of woman. They are present-day manifestations of the original Image of God brought into being at the Beginning of time, before Adam. In accordance with this imagery, they are not born of woman.

Thomas takes it for granted that there was a period of perfect original time from the Beginning to Adam, during which God's Image came into being but was not born of woman. This was followed by a second period, from sexually divided and fallen Adam to John the Baptist, when being born of woman was inevitable and invariable, and then a final period after John (implicitly a period beginning with Jesus), when humans could again return to the status of the Beginning, be reborn as metaphorical infants, and regain the condition of not being born of woman.

59 This is a series of proverbial sayings listed together without intervening "Jesus said" separators. The proverb at 47c is obviously true for anyone who has a taste for good wine. One does not sip wine of a good vintage and then request a glass of gallon-jug red. The word "wine" brought to Thomas's mind another proverb regarding new and vintage wine, which also shows familiarity with wine's characteristics. If fresh wine swells or emits gases, inflexible old wineskins will burst; new wineskins that are not fully cured will inevitably convey taste to vintage wine and spoil its delicate flavor.

But the concluding proverb here, 47e, gets it wrong. The canonical version, found at Mark 3:21, reads "no one sews a piece of unshrunk cloth on an old garment..." and goes on to explain that when the new cloth is wetted and subsequently shrinks, it will tear away from the old, which is true to life. But the opposite is not true; it is not the case that a patch of old cloth will tear away when sewn to a new garment. A careless copyist is probably at fault here.

46a Jesus said: From Adam to John the Baptist, no one born of a woman is above John the Baptist, so that he should not lower his eyes.

46b But I have said: Whoever among you becomes like an infant will know the Kingdom and be greater than John.[58]

47a Jesus said: One person cannot ride two horses at once, nor stretch two bows,

47b nor can a servant serve two masters, as he will respect one and despise the other.

47c No one drinks vintage wine and immediately wants to drink fresh wine.

47d Fresh wine is not put into old wineskins because they might burst. Vintage wine is not put into new wineskins because it might be spoiled.

47e A patch of old cloth is not sewn onto a new garment because it would tear.[59]

60 A saying found in Matthew 18:19, "I tell you that if two of you on earth agree about anything you ask for, it will be done for you by my Father in heaven," echoes the theme found here in Thomas 48. It seems to have been the custom for itinerant Christians to offer "peace" to householders. We hear in Luke 10:5–6, "When you enter a house, first say, 'Peace to this house.' If a man of peace is there, your peace will rest on him; if not, it will return to you." Thomas 48 presupposes a time when two *have* successfully made peace in a house. The main point of the saying emphasizes how difficult it is for two people living together to find peace; yet, if they are able to do so they can then do anything.

61 We should be careful not to assume automatically that the Kingdom occupies some other part of space so that coming from the Kingdom involves coming down from somewhere. Thomas's saying 3 sarcastically mocks those who would place the Kingdom somewhere above. The Kingdom is fundamentally temporal rather than spatial, it is a time, and that time is the Beginning. So to come from the Kingdom is not to come from a place or dimension but to come from the time of the Beginning. Accordingly, returning to the Kingdom from which you came is the same as returning to the Beginning at which you originated, as sayings 18 and 19 emphasize.

Time running backward produces ever-younger people, until finally one reaches again the state of infancy. To continue backward would bring one ultimately to the Beginning of the world. In the sayings of the Gospel of Thomas, this regression of time is one of the most important recurring motifs. Strikingly absent, however, are any clear directions on how to accomplish such a regression in time; the secret to that is evidently hidden within the person and within the world, hidden along with the Kingdom of Heaven.

48 Jesus said: If two can make peace between themselves in a single house, they can say to a mountain, "Move!" and it will move.[60]

49 Jesus said: Blessed are the single ones and the chosen ones, for you will find the Kingdom. Because you emerged from it you will return to it.[61]

62 Who are "they"? Obviously, "they" are people. Perhaps they are authorities directing a Christian ritual in which questions and answers are exchanged. Thomas 50 might therefore be something of a catechism. On the other hand, "they" may be people outside the community who have heard about aspects of Thomasine belief, and missionaries are being told how to answer their questions.

Saying 50a is literally impossible to understand. The key elements are the referents of the pronouns, and we do not know what each pronoun refers to. Revealed in "their image"? We have no way of knowing what that means because we have no answer to "they who?" "It came" or "He came"? Who? This is incomprehensible. It presupposes that the reader knows things the reader cannot know. Light was first produced at the outset of creation, as the first sentences of Genesis reveal, so 50a, like 49, may speak of "coming from a place" that should be understood to be "emerging at a time."

Saying 50b reflects the idea of chosen-ness that is also found in sayings 23 and 49. It recalls the idea of Sonship found in saying 3, where we are told that people are already Sons of the living Father and that the greater struggle is to become able to realize that fact. It is significant that the Thomasine Christians do not reserve the idea of divine Sonship uniquely to Jesus. It also applies to themselves. Similarly, in Paul's letter to the Galatians (4:6–7), he declares that all who receive the Spirit of the Son become God's Sons.

Saying 50c might possibly refer to Genesis 1. There creation begins with movement as the Spirit moves upon the waters (1:2) and concludes with rest on the seventh day, the Sabbath of God (2:2). If Thomas's sayings call people back to that perfect Kingdom of creation of the first seven days, then their sign of the Father might be movement and rest.

50a Jesus said: If they ask you, "Where are you from?" reply to them, "We have come from the place where light is produced from itself. It came and revealed itself in their image."

50b If they ask you, "Are you it?" reply to them, "We are his Sons. We are chosen ones of the living Father."

50c If they ask you "What is the sign within you of your Father?" reply to them, "It is movement. It is rest."[62]

63 These two questions, along with the questions introducing the next two sayings, 52 and 53, require answers that establish basic principles concerning some of the most fundamental issues in the lives of early Christians. The present saying straightforwardly addresses the question whether the teachings of Jesus are to be understood as predictions of the future end of this world and its replacement by a better world, or whether his teachings were oriented to the present. Here the disciples ask questions about themselves, as individuals concerned with "rest" (which we can safely assume is the equivalent of eternal life) and about the future coming of the new world. Interest in the predicted future is typical of the Christianity of Mark, Matthew, and Luke—and, for that matter, the letters of Paul. But it is not typical of John's Gospel or of the Gospel of Thomas.

The first question focuses on individuals who have sought rest for themselves, and the second question concerns humanity as a whole, all of whom, it is assumed, will be affected when the Kingdom arrives. In response, Jesus gives one reply, which is that the dead rest *now* instead of having to wait for an undetermined interim period, and that the new world has *already* arrived. Indeed, it has been here since the opening days of creation, for the seven days of Genesis 1 did not cease to be when the creation of Genesis 2 came into being, even if the Fall blinded Adam, the man of dust of the second creation, to the glories of the first creation.

51 His disciples asked him: When will the dead rest? When will the new world arrive? He replied: That which you are waiting for has come, but you don't recognize it.[63]

64 The statement that initiates saying 52 addresses a matter of immense concern to New Testament–era Christians: whether there is evidence that Jesus is the man of great importance that Christians believe him to be and, if so, how others can be convinced by that evidence. One mode of argument, found throughout the New Testament, is commonly called "proof from prophecy." It claims that the ancient prophets of the Hebrew Bible predicted events that would occur in the life of the Messiah. It is then asserted that these events did in fact occur in the career of Jesus. Naturally, evangelists went out of their way to include such events in their narratives. It follows, so they believed, that Jesus was thereby proved to be the Messiah.

Here, in the Gospel of Thomas, Jesus speaks against this whole idea, saying that the prophets, twenty-four of whom were indeed traditionally considered to be the authors of the prophetic canonical scriptures, are not to be considered a source of authority in regard to Jesus. They may or may not have spoken of Jesus, but that is rejected as a relevant point of argument. Jesus' answer directs the reader to the present day. Perhaps "the living one" is Jesus; perhaps it is the presence of "the living one" within the light that indwells any Christian. The existence of "the living one" *now* is the main point made here. Saying 51 opened with a dual question about the future. This saying begins with a statement that refers to the past. In both cases, Jesus' responses reject the presuppositions of the questions and point to the present day. Everything that needs to be sought and found is here now. The dead past and the imaginary future are irrelevant.

52 They said to him: Twenty-four prophets spoke to Israel, and they all spoke of you. He responded to them: You have deserted the living one who is with you, and you spoke about the dead.[64]

65 This question, third in a list of topics very important to first-century Christians, has to do with the symbolic entry requirement for males interested in joining the Jewish religion. One sees in Paul's letters that circumcision was symbolic of the agreement to keep Torah as a whole. It was (and is) to Judaism what baptism is to Christianity: a ritual that initiated babies and adults into the religion and symbolized the adoption of the religion. A question concerning circumcision features a single part that signifies the whole. So the greater question would be: "Is keeping the Torah, the law of Judea, required or not?"

Jesus was a Galilean. A Galilean was not a Judean. A Galilean did not necessarily value the customs or treasure the laws of Judea. Here in saying 53 Jesus sarcastically condemns the practice of circumcision. Thomas's saying advocates circumcision of the spirit, as did Paul, who wrote in Romans 2:28: "He is a Jew who is one inwardly, and real circumcision is a matter of the heart, spiritual and not literal." Accordingly, Paul and Thomas are alike in the belief that Christians are free of the Jewish Judean law.

66 Jesus may well have spoken this famous beatitude intending to announce the blessings of poverty-stricken people, individuals without money, but it seems likely that the context of the Gospel of Thomas brings a different meaning to this saying. The poor are probably people who have put aside the worldly things that Thomas's Gospel calls "the world" and have done so as part of the quest to find the Kingdom of Heaven.

53 His disciples asked him: Is circumcision useful or not? He replied: If it were useful, then they would be born already circumcised. On the other hand, true circumcision in the spirit is entirely beneficial.[65]

54 Jesus said: Blessed are the poor, for yours is the Kingdom of Heaven.[66]

67 This strikingly peculiar statement is echoed in other places in the early Christian tradition. We find a very similar version in Luke's Gospel: "If anyone comes to me and does not hate his own father and mother and wife and children and brothers and sisters, yes, and even his own life, he cannot be my disciple" (14:26). Here the family by marriage is added to the listed members of the family by birth.

Anyone who thinks about the life of Jesus and his disciples realizes that those men, and the "many women" (Matthew 27:55, Luke 8:1–3, Mark 15:41) who were with them, deserted their own families to move with Jesus through Galilee and Judea. Who was taking care of their relatives in their absence? What happened to the wives and parents and children left behind when disciples left everything to follow him? We don't know, of course, but the severing of familial bonds in practice presumably was coupled with the severing of emotional bonds as well.

The final element in saying 55 about "bear his cross as I do" is the only place in the whole of the Gospel of Thomas where a cross is mentioned. In the ancient sayings list that scholars call Q, which the great majority of New Testament scholars believe was used by Matthew and Luke in the production of their gospels, the only time a cross is mentioned is in this very same saying. Neither Thomas nor Q shows any interest whatsoever in what later Christian orthodoxy came to regard as the most crucial elements of the Christian religion: Jesus' death and resurrection. That implies that there were significant branches of early Christianity that focused exclusively on Jesus as a teacher rather than on Jesus as a sacrifice or as a prototype for Christians' resurrection.

55 Jesus said: He who doesn't hate his father and mother cannot be a disciple of mine. He who doesn't hate his brothers and sisters and bear his cross as I do will not be worthy of me.[67]

68 The praise formula at the end of this saying, "the world is not worthy of him," means that "whoever has known the world" has done exactly the right thing. Then, how does one properly know the world? Evidently by discovering that the world is, in some respect, a corpse. A corpse, however, is a body that has previously been animated. A rock is not a corpse. To properly find the world, then, would seem to require one to separate the world as animate from the world as inanimate, and so to discover not only in what respect the world seems to be a corpse unanimated, but also to discover what it was that potentially animates it. If Thomas has in mind the world's two creations, and believes that the first is the Kingdom of Heaven hidden in the world, then perhaps the second creation alone (Genesis 2:4–5:1), in the absence of the first, is to be likened to a corpse. The world is a corpse because it lacks an animating principle. Is this its permanent state? From the perspective of the Gospel of Thomas, it seems that the animating principle of the world is the Kingdom within it that remains undiscovered by most people. They do not realize that for them the world is a corpse; when they discover that it is, they simultaneously discover the Kingdom that can animate it.

❖ "The Gospel of Thomas is the product of an autonomous tradition. Of this one may be sure. Put in the most general terms, it belongs to the same period of Christian writing that produced the canonical gospels. Of this, too, one may be confident. As such, it stands as a relatively new and independent witness to the complex and obscure period of Christian origins. Whatever we may learn about the persons who used and championed it, about their relationship to other early Christian groups, and about their theology will be of obvious value in the continuing endeavor to understand the elusive reality of Christian beginnings."

—Stephen J. Patterson, *The Gospel of Thomas and Jesus*, p. 121

56 Jesus said: Whoever has known the world has found a corpse; whoever has found that corpse, the world is not worthy of him.[68]

69 The main actor appears at first glance to be God or Jesus, and one assumes almost automatically that those supernatural beings necessarily do what is best. But that common assumption makes readers miss the parable's main point. If we do not automatically assume that the main actor, the farmer who sows seed, is divine, then his actions are incompetent. If it were that easy, that's what we would all do. We would not weed our gardens or make the effort to learn what young weeds look like, but we would wait until all the plants were fully grown and then pull out the obvious weeds. But then it would be far too late; the weeds already would have taken the moisture and nutrition and sunlight from the domesticated plants throughout the whole growing season. To avoid this is why we weed in the first place. By the time of harvest, weeds are irrelevant, for they have done their damage already, and cutting them down and burning them will no longer serve any purpose.

Possibly the point of this parable has to do with the lack of wisdom of the main actor who fails to understand the basic principles of competent farming. Jesus, from rural Galilee, probably knew farming rather well, as did his mostly rural audiences. This parable shares a principal element, a farmer acting incompetently, with the parable of the sower, discussed previously as saying 9. There the farmer scatters seed randomly, most of which is wasted and unproductive.

70 Individuals are commanded to take action on their own behalf, and those who do so successfully receive a blessing that is not due to the pure unaided grace of God. In keeping with the Gospel of Thomas's general tendency toward evasiveness and indirection, we are not told exactly how to go about laboring. Evidently it culminates in "finding" life, so the labor in question is the "seeking" advocated elsewhere in this Gospel. The challenge appears to be to investigate the sayings of Jesus preserved here so as to derive a new overall comprehension of the world as the place of the Kingdom of Heaven and of oneself as the location of the light that illuminates that Kingdom. The sayings of Thomas as a whole, then, are the beginning point of a "seeking" that moves one within oneself and outside into the world, finally to culminate in "finding" life and receiving blessing.

57 Jesus said: The Kingdom of the Father is like a man with good seed. His enemy came at night and scattered the seed of weeds in with the good seed. The man did not let them pull out the weeds but said, "Don't do it. You might pull out the grain along with the weeds." During the harvest the weeds will be obvious, and then they can be removed and burned.[69]

58 Jesus said: Blessed is one who has labored and has found life.[70]

71 The "living one" is not necessarily Jesus. The "living one" could be God, and therefore individuals can be called "Sons of the living Father," as in saying 3. Or possibly the "living one" is the light that exists within individuals, within the sons of the living one. In that case, saying 59 directs people toward self-discovery during their lives, for the self-discovery of the living one within oneself must happen before death.

72 This is a puzzling saying, or rather a vignette. It is one of the very few passages in Thomas that is even remotely like the story-telling narratives of the canonical gospels. Here an event occurs, and Jesus responds to that event by initiating a dialogue with his disciples. Thomas's Gospel hardly ever has such scenes.

Everyone knows that animals are killed and eaten by people and that no one eats living animals. Why, then, is this being pointed out to us with such care by Jesus in this vignette? At the conclusion of the dialogue, we hear that unless you seek and find a place of rest you will become a corpse, which is a very similar observation to that of the previous saying, 59, telling us that unless you find the living one while you live you will die and be unable to do so. "Do it before you die" doesn't seem like advice people couldn't have figured out by themselves. It seems to imply that there is a potential audience whose members believe that progress can be made after one dies, that "finding rest" or "looking to the living one" can potentially occur in an afterlife. Sayings 59 and 60 deny this. In so doing, they may be denying the belief that became standard Christian doctrine: that one's encounter with God and one's divine rest occur after death in heaven. If you must find the living one and find rest now, anticipating it later in heaven would indeed be a mistake.

59 Jesus said: Look at the living one while you live, for if you die and then try to see him you will not be able to do so.[71]

60 They saw a Samaritan going into Judea carrying a lamb. He asked his disciples: What do you think he will do with that lamb? They replied: He'll kill it and eat it. He said to them: As long as it remains alive he will not eat it; only if he kills it and it becomes a corpse. They said: Otherwise he won't be able to do so. He said to them: You too must seek a place for rest, or you may become a corpse and be eaten.[72]

73 Saying 61a appears to be a proverb counseling resignation in the face of unpredictable disasters. Our culture's proverb "some you win, some you lose" is similar. There is no good reason to separate 61a from saying 60, where it could just as well be labeled 60b. Or, indeed, it could easily have been numbered as a separate unit. One must bear in mind that the numbering in Thomas's Gospel is an arbitrary modern convention that should not govern one's interpretation of the sayings.

Saying 61b is another of Thomas's rare vignettes, one probably called to mind by the vignette in the passage immediately preceding it, saying 60. This vignette and its dialogue have been garbled in transmission. Accurate translation would require knowledge of words that have dropped out through copyists' errors. The scene evidently takes place in the home of Salome, whose name is found in the Gospel of Mark as one of the women who saw where Jesus was buried and who went to anoint his body.

Saying 61c contrasts light and darkness in a manner that is common throughout the world's religions and can be found in texts of the Dead Sea Scrolls where the "sons of light" strive against the "sons of darkness." Only through singleness, *monachos*, can a person be unified, integrated, and whole and discover light within. Such a person can, in accord with saying 24, illuminate the whole world. One who is divided is in darkness and cannot shine.

❖ "It is probable that many of the sayings in the Gospel of Thomas which are not preserved elsewhere also derive from early traditions of sayings of Jesus. This document is, therefore, an important source of as well as witness to Jesus' sayings. Since the Gospel of Thomas is independent of the writings of the New Testament, its date of composition is not contingent upon these or any other written documents we now possess. Its earliest possible date of composition would be in the middle of the first century, when other sayings collections first began to be compiled."

—Ron Cameron, *The Other Gospels: Non-Canonical Gospel Texts*, p. 24

61a Jesus said: Two will lie down on one bed; one will die and the other will live.

61b Salome asked him: Who are you, man? As though coming from someone, you have come onto my couch and eaten from my table. Jesus replied: I am he who comes into being from him who is the same. Some of the things of my Father have been given to me. Salome said: I am your disciple.

61c Therefore I say that if one is unified one will be filled with light, but if one is divided one will be filled with darkness.[73]

74 Saying 62a may be the conclusion of saying 61, for there Jesus entered into a dialogue with Salome, to whom he revealed a mystery: "if one is unified one will be filled with light, but if one is divided one will be filled with darkness." Accordingly, Salome and Thomas (saying 13) are the two people named in the Gospel as being worthy of Jesus' mysteries.

In the Gospel of Thomas, Jesus reveals his mysteries obliquely, indirectly, through parables and proverbs and obscure statements. Those worthy of the mysteries, therefore, are those who have proved themselves able to fathom them, seek their meaning, and find their interpretation. Jesus does not reveal his mysteries to you; he reveals the opportunity for you to find the meaning of those mysteries on your own.

75 This is a parable, a very brief story that makes a single point, but it is not a parable similar to most of those attributed to Jesus. The striking features of Jesus' parables—and they are, arguably, unique—is that they twist the hearer's apprehensions, contain an element of surprise, and generally are difficult to understand fully. But this parable is simple, its meaning is absolutely straightforward, and it could have come from any culture. Its point, of course, is that the accumulation of worldly goods is only temporarily satisfying in face of inevitable death. Or, as we say, "you can't take it with you." Ironically, in the vocabulary of saying 3, the rich man lives in metaphorical "poverty."

62a Jesus said: I tell my mysteries to people worthy of my mysteries.[74]

62b Do not let your left hand know what your right hand is doing.

63 Jesus said: Once there was a rich man who had lots of money, and he said, "I will invest my money so that I can sow, reap, plant, and fill up my silos with crops so that I won't lack anything." So he thought, but that night he died. He who has ears, let him hear.[75]

76 The odd thing about this story—an oddness that fits the obscure style of a typical Jesus parable in a way that the clarity of the preceding parable 62 does not—is that this host acts irrationally. He has ordered the full dinner prepared, and only when it is done does he send his servant to see whether any of his guests will actually show up to eat it. It turns out that they cannot. All the guests give quite reasonable excuses that make perfectly good sense in an ancient world context. Deuteronomy 20:5–8 lists a set of acceptable excuses that are generally similar in nature, but different in detail, to the excuses the invitees offer here. The host is left with a fully prepared meal. Because of his tardiness in determining who will come for it, either he must throw it out or invite random strangers to dine. He does the latter.

Often this parable is interpreted as an invitation by God to humanity, one favoring the less fortunate over the well-to-do. But the host does not make a careful choice between his erstwhile friends and his invitation to people at random; rather he is forced into this choice against his will. If he had had his way, his wealthy friends would be in attendance, but because of what appears to be his own lack of planning, he finds himself stuck with a crowd of strangers. The point of the parable may be to hold up the host as an example of one who has failed to think things through.

77 Saying 64b is one of the few places where a compiler or a later scribe of the Gospel of Thomas has added a saying for the purpose of leading readers to interpret a saying in a particular way. Here the rather curt dismissive, "Merchants and salesmen will not enter the places of my Father," serves to interpret the parable's host as "my Father" and to insist that those invited symbolize "merchants and salesmen," even though the excuses the guests offer appear to be perfectly valid.

64a Jesus said: A man entertained guests. When dinner was ready he sent a servant to invite his guests. The servant went to the first one and said, "My master invites you," but he replied, "I have to collect money from some merchants, and they are due to arrive this evening. Therefore I have to do business with them, and I must be excused from the dinner." The servant went to another and said, "My master invites you," but he said, "I have just bought a house, and I have to spend a day there, so I cannot come. I must be excused." He went to the next and said, "My master invites you." This one replied, "My friend is about to be married, and I must organize the dinner. I can't come. I must be excused." Again he went and said to another, "My master invites you." He replied, "I have just bought a village, and I have to go collect the rent. I can't come and must be excused." The servant reported back to his master, "Those whom you invited to the dinner are unable to come." The master said, "Go to the roads outside and invite anybody you can find to the dinner."[76]

64b Merchants and salesmen will not enter the places of my Father.[77]

78 This parable presents the same problem as several others do, for the landowner acts in an incompetent and ultimately disastrous manner. What sane man would discover that his tenants violently refuse to pay up, that they have beaten his first agent nearly to death and a second agent also, and then send his son and heir into the same situation? But that is what the landlord does in this case. His reward is to have his son murdered. This is a man who does not learn from experience. The idea that the landlord represents God and the son represents Christ is not present in Thomas's Gospel.

79 Saying 66 sounds like a proverb, one akin to our references to the ugly duckling who grew to be a swan. It appears in the Hebrew Bible, where Psalm 118:22 reads, "I thank you that you have answered me and have become my salvation. The stone which the builders rejected has become the head of the corner." There are few Hebrew scripture quotations in the Gospel of Thomas, but this is certainly one of them.

65 He said: A good man had a vineyard that he arranged for tenant farmers to take care of for him in return for a portion of the produce. He sent a servant to collect the grapes. Tenants seized the servant and beat him nearly to death. That servant reported back to his master, but his master responded, "Perhaps they did not recognize him." And so he sent another servant; the tenants beat him too. Then the owner sent his own son, saying, "Perhaps they will show some respect for my son." Since the tenants were aware that he would inherit the vineyard, they seized him and then killed him. He who has ears, let him hear.[78]

66 Jesus said: Show me the stone that the builders rejected. It is the cornerstone.[79]

80 The Gospel of Thomas conceives of the Kingdom of Heaven as existing within people and outside of them. Finding it is the goal of human life, a guarantor of immortality. Its discovery comes from illuminating the world with light from within oneself. If one does not know oneself, one does not have access to one's light. In turn, lack of access to the light keeps one from illuminating the Kingdom within the world. First and foremost, therefore, one must know oneself. To substitute knowledge in general for self-knowledge is completely misguided.

81 It is puzzling why so much very early Christian literature assumes that persecution is an inherent part of being a Christian. The ancient world was by no means a place where well-defined doctrinal parameters defined orthodoxy and heresy so that dissenters would regularly be persecuted for their beliefs. The violent suppression of religious ideas became characteristic of Western religions only in later centuries.

In the earliest period, whatever Christians were doing, they did in the cultural region of Judea and Judaism. Paul describes his own career at the beginning of his Letter to the Galatians. First, he tells us, he "advanced in Judaism beyond many of my own age among my people, so extremely zealous was I for the traditions of my fathers" (Galatians 1:14), by which he means the Judean Torah law. At this time (and we can guess that he was in his very early twenties), he "persecuted the church of God violently and tried to destroy it" (1:13).

Paul never puts forth the factors that motivated his persecution of Christians, but it seems very unlikely that matters of religious opinion were at issue. Probably persecution arose because at least some Judean, Galilean, and Syrian Christians took the principles we see in sayings 14 and 53 quite seriously and did not fast or pray or circumcise. They did not follow Judean law and encouraged others not to. That would certainly have motivated persecutors from the ranks of those Judeans who were zealous for the traditions.

67 Jesus said: One who knows everything else but who does not know himself knows nothing.[80]

68 Jesus said: Blessed are you when they hate and persecute you. No place will be found where they persecuted you.[81]

82 The first of these beatitudes, so called because *beatus* is the Latin word for "blessing," changes the focus from the external persecution suggested in saying 68 toward an internal persecution. Why would self-persecution bring about knowledge of the Father? Possibly because Thomas's gospel advocates that people change their self-awareness. In saying 67, difficult though it is to render intelligibly, what seems to be at issue is self-knowledge. Self-knowledge famously entails honest self-appraisal, and that seems inevitably to lead to suffering. So one's persecution of oneself probably involves the process of awakening to true self-knowledge, and that in turn brings about illumination from the light that is within, as Thomas's saying 24 indicates. Unfortunately for us all, when the inner light is kindled, what lies within to be illuminated is not always what we wish to be there.

83 Saying 69b, another beatitude, resolutely focuses on the present, citing deliberate generosity rather than accidental poverty as the reason for the hunger. Simply being hungry does not bring blessing, but hungering because one has generously given to others who hunger—that does bring blessing.

❖ "For the Thomas Christian, to know the Reign of God is to know one's true identity as 'children of the Living Father.' This reign cannot be associated with a future event, as though one's true identity as a child of God is something that will be revealed only at some future time. Nor can it be associated solely with a transcendent realm, as though this identity cannot be realized even in the midst of life's concrete situations. In the Gospel of Thomas, the presence of the Reign of God here and now represents a radical insistence upon the true identity and grounding of human being in God, a fact which the presence of the world or the nature of the present age cannot be allowed to obstruct."

—Stephen Patterson, "Introduction," in *Q-Thomas Reader*, edited by John Kloppenborg, p. 100

69a Jesus said: Blessed are those who have been persecuted within themselves. They have really come to know the Father.[82]

69b Blessed are those who are hungry in order to fill the bellies of the needy.[83]

84 This saying brings to mind saying 24, where we hear that "There is light within a man of light, and he lights up all of the world. If he is not alight there is darkness," for this gives an answer to the question "what is it that is within?" From the context of Thomas, the answer is "light." If that light is understood in terms of some ancient theories of vision, it is not simply light serving as a metaphor for self-understanding or divine wisdom. Rather, it is light that emerges from a person into the world so as to illuminate the world and make the world visible.

The Gospel of Thomas presents the idea that the world can be comprehended in either of two fashions. You can see it in the usual way, the standard mode of human perception from the time of fallen Adam to the present day, or you can see the world in the light of the first day of creation, when light came forth from God. It seems reasonable to assume that this is the light used by the Image of God to perceive the world during the prototypical first seven days. If people can see the world in the actual light of the first days, then they see it as the Kingdom of Heaven, but if they see it in the ordinary light of everyday experience, then they do not see the Kingdom of Heaven at all.

So, what is within a person is the supernal light of creation. If it shines, it brings with it the Kingdom and eternal life: if it does not shine, the world is darkness. If the world is darkness, then it is death, and what you have failed to light up will destroy you. According to saying 70, your destruction is under your own control, as is your salvation.

70 Jesus said: When you give rise to that which is within you, what you have will save you. If you do not give rise to it, what you do not have will destroy you.[84]

85 It is practically impossible to say what this sentence means. It seems to have arisen from a particular occasion in Jesus' life, one about which we know nothing. If we imagine that it is meant literally, then Jesus intends to destroy a house and order that it cannot be rebuilt. Is it a "leprous" house, one with a spreading discoloration that must be ordered destroyed in accordance with Leviticus 14:34–47? Probably not, because the diagnosis of house leprosy must be made by a priest, and Jesus, of course, was not a priest. Should we understand the "house" to be a symbol for the Jerusalem temple? There is certainly no saying within the Gospel of Thomas that supports that symbolic meaning. In fact, the Gospel of Thomas never mentions the temple at all, positively or negatively.

86 This simple dialogue portrays Jesus as reacting in a rather snippy fashion to what appears to be a reasonable request. It is evidently meant to be something of a joke, and as such is one of the very few attempts at humor in Christian tradition. It is a play on words. The Jesus of the Gospel of Thomas advocates oneness, singleness, unity. For example, in saying 61c we hear "if one is unified one will be filled with light, but if one is divided one will be filled with darkness." Now he is asked to advocate division. How ironic, we are supposed to think, and how inappropriate.

❖ "The spirituality implied in the Gospel of Thomas is a type of unitive mysticism. The theme of unity runs through the document as a whole. In two sayings it replaces the synoptic 'faith' as the force which removes mountains (sayings 48 and 106)."

—H.E.W. Turner, *Thomas and the Evangelists* (London: Allenson, 1962), p. 105

71 Jesus said: I will destroy this house, and no one will be able to build it again.[85]

72 A man said to him: Talk to my brothers so that they will divide my father's property with me. Jesus replied: Man, who made me a divider? He turned to his disciples and asked them: Really, am I a divider?[86]

87 If we look at this set of statements as a dialogue, the first unit, Jesus' statement, simply remarks on a present lack of workers. There is nothing here to imply that the master is an allegory for God or that the harvest symbolizes the Christian mission. The anonymous responder then says, in effect, that there are many potential workers but none willing to do the difficult job; he contrasts people drinking water with the absence of people willing to get into the well to ensure the provision of water. He may have meant, "Many are available but few actually show up."

At the end of the sequence we find an interpretive summary that moves the discussion from the mundane realm of the harvest into the spiritual realm of symbolic reality. The word "single" reflects the idea of unification and oneness. Oneness is likened to a single person entering a bridal suite. In the symbolic bridal suite, a single person becomes a Single One on a higher level. In other words, as Mark puts it in his gospel, (10:6–8) "a man shall leave his father and mother and be joined to his wife, and the two shall become one. So they are no longer two but one," citing ideas that refer back to Genesis 2:44 and the (re)union of Adam and Eve. So too, in the Gospel of Thomas people are encouraged to achieve unity and singleness within themselves so that they may enter the bridal chamber, where the two shall become one in a more supernatural dimension. Thomas does not ever discuss the union within the bridal suite in more detail, although the bridal suite is mentioned again in saying 104.

88 Unless we are familiar with the canonical sayings, we would not automatically assume that the long-lasting treasures that do not decay, mentioned in saying 76b, are supernatural heavenly treasures. That would be one interpretation, but it would not be the only possible one. For example, precious metals would meet the criteria stated in 76b. So, significantly, would pearls, and that fact may have led to the combination of two separate sayings into one saying.

73 Jesus said: The harvest is great, but there are only a few workers. Ask the master to send more workers for the harvest. (74) He said: Master, there are many around the drinking barrel, but there is nobody in the well. (75) Jesus said: There are many standing by the door, but only the single will enter the bridal suite.[87]

76a Jesus said: The Kingdom of the Father is like a merchant with goods to sell who found a pearl. The merchant was thoughtful. He sold the merchandise and bought himself the pearl.

76b You too should seek for long-lasting treasures that do not decay, where moths do not come to eat them or grubs to destroy them.[88]

89 This is one of the most striking sayings in the Gospel of Thomas, and it is one of the very few pantheistic (God-is-all-things) sayings found anywhere in the early Christian tradition. Of all the sayings in the Gospel of Thomas, this saying, 77a, is most similar to the style of sayings found in the Gospel of John, where we hear Jesus say, "I am the way and the truth and the life" (John 14:6), "I am the bread of life" (6:48), and, most significantly, "I am the light of the world" (8:12, 9:5).

The idea that all things came forth from Jesus is similar to ideas found elsewhere in early Christian writing, for example, 1 Corinthians 8:6: "For us there is...one Lord, Jesus Christ, through whom are all things and through whom we exist," and Hebrews 1:1–3: "In many and various ways God spoke of old to our fathers by the prophets; but in these last days he has spoken to us by a Son, whom he has appointed the heir of all things, through whom also he created the world," and Colossians 1:15–16: "He is the image of the invisible God, the first-born of all creation; for in him all things were created in heaven and on earth...all things were created through him and for him." The most famous passage of this sort is John 1:1–3: "In the beginning was the Word and the Word was with God, and the Word was God. He was in the beginning with God; all things were made through him, and without him was not anything made that was made." Saying 77a fits well within the pattern of thought of these early Christian poems, for they all affirm the creative power of Jesus in the beginning of creation.

90 Saying 77b was moved by a scribe from where it first was located in Greek Thomas, at the end of saying 30, to its present location at the end of saying 77. This saying, or rather, one based on it, gained a considerable amount of fame when it was repeatedly used in the 1999 Hollywood film *Stigmata*. The *Stigmata* version combines the thought of Thomas's saying 3a with words from saying 77b and shows the influence of a phrase attributed to Stephen in Acts 7:48: "The Most High does not dwell in houses made with hands." The actual wording in the movie itself varies from one instance to another, again showing

(continued on page 100)

77a Jesus said: I am the light above everything. I am everything. Everything came forth from me, and everything reached me.[89]

77b Split wood, I am there. Lift up a rock, you will find me there.[90]

the inevitable changes that occur when sayings are transmitted, but it comes down to this: "The Kingdom of God is inside/within you (and all about you), not in buildings/mansions of wood and stone. (When I am gone) Split a piece of wood and I am there, lift the/a stone and you will find me." The Thomasine community would have approved of this saying wholeheartedly, for it speaks of the presence of the Kingdom of Heaven throughout this world.

91 In this saying, Jesus speaks about his own location and appearance. The audience has gone into the desert to see Jesus, and they are not entirely satisfied with what they found. Presumably they found Jesus dressed in rags. He responds angrily that if they have come to the desert to see someone dressed elegantly, they have come to the wrong place, just as if they had come to see reeds shaken by the wind. Reeds, of course, are not desert plants but littoral plants growing on the banks of lakes and streams. Jesus contrasts himself—in the desert, socially outcast—with elegantly dressed kings and courtiers, who live in the well-watered regions where reeds can be found. The truth is evidently to be discovered outside the margins of established society. His audience might come to know the truth, but only if they are willing to accept what they do find in the desert and stop wishing that they had found something else.

92 In saying 79a, Jesus modestly deflects praise from his mother, and indirectly himself, toward the general category of those who are obedient to God. Saying 79b is a warning of disaster to come, when children will be much more a burden than a blessing, but whether that disaster is to be understood in a political-warfare sense or in an end-of-the-present-world sense is impossible to determine.

78 Jesus said: Why did you go into the desert? Did you expect to see reeds shaken by the wind? To see people clothed in elegant garments like your kings and courtiers? They wear elegant garments and cannot know the truth.[91]

79a A woman in the crowd said to him: Blessed are the womb that bore you and the breasts that nourished you. He replied: Blessed are those who have listened to the word of the Father and really done it.

79b For the days are coming when you will say "Blessed are the womb that has never conceived and the breasts that have never given milk."[92]

93 Thomas's sayings often encourage seeking and finding, although they are deliberately obscure about to how to seek and what to find. It appears that the world can be apprehended in two ways, either as the ordinary world of present circumstances or as a place containing an indwelling secret Kingdom of Heaven present in it from the Beginning. Coming to know the world means coming to know the Kingdom within the world, said here to be the same as finding the body. Saying 80 is a variation on saying 56, which speaks of finding a corpse and that "the world is not worthy" of one who has found that corpse. "Corpse" in Greek is *ptoma* and "body" is *soma;* the Thomas sayings separately use each. There is an implied equation: World is to Body as Kingdom is to Spirit. Accordingly, to find the body is to find that which contains the spirit; in other words, to find the world is to find the Kingdom within the world.

80 Jesus said: Whoever has come to know the world has found the body. Whoever has found that body, the world is not worthy of him.[93]

94 Saying 2 tells us that the seeker will seek and then find, then be disturbed and astonished, and then finally reign or rule over everything, which fits the role of the Image of God during the first seven days, when humanity is given the charge to rule over all the creatures of the earth (Genesis 1:26). Saying 3b uses poverty as the opposite of self-knowledge. Accordingly, poverty's opposite, riches, should be the equivalent metaphor for the attainment of self-knowledge: "If you do not know yourselves, then you exist in poverty and you are that poverty." If you do know yourselves, then presumably you are wealthy and you are that wealth. In the context of these sayings, "whoever has become rich should rule" makes good symbolic sense as an admonition to self-knowledge that returns one to the condition of the primordial humanity described in Genesis 1:26. It is not necessary to bring into consideration the United States Congress.

The final clause of saying 81 may indicate that those who have found self-knowledge and who metaphorically rule ought not think that this automatically entitles them to political authority within the movement. In Mark's Gospel Jesus similarly says, paradoxically, "whoever would be great among you must be your servant" (10:43).

95 Sometimes in the Gospel of Thomas, those who focus especially on the person of Jesus himself are frowned upon, but here in saying 82, as in saying 77, we find a strong Christological emphasis. In saying 77, Jesus is the origin of all things, present in all things; now, in saying 82, he is fire and Kingdom both. The implicit identification of "fire" and "Kingdom" is interesting. Something of the same idea is present in saying 10 as well: "I have thrown fire on the world. Look! I watch it until it blazes." Saying 10 implies a radical near-future change coming in the form of a cosmic conflagration sparked by Jesus himself. In accordance with saying 10, where Jesus has control of the fire that will soon blaze, saying 82 almost identifies that fire with Jesus and certainly identifies that fire with the Kingdom. One might therefore re-read saying 10 as "I have thrown the Kingdom on the world."

81 Jesus said: Whoever has become rich should rule.
Whoever has power should renounce it.[94]

82 Jesus said: Whoever is near to me is near the fire.
Whoever is far from me is far from the Kingdom.[95]

96 These two "sayings" appear to be somewhat garbled passages from an ancient religio-philosophical document; they do not sound as if they come from conversational speech. If we assume that the technical term "images" implies a Platonic philosophical perspective, the images in saying 83 are the things of this world, which are in reality only images of true ideal things existing in another more exalted world. On the exalted level, ideals exist as they have since the primordial Beginning, when God declared them permanently good. Insofar as things exist in relationship to the Beginning, they exist in the realm of the Father's light, for the Genesis story begins on the first day with "Let there be light" and continues, on the fourth day, to give an account of the creation of the stars, sun, and moon. Therefore, the light of the first day is a completely different sort of light from earthly light. God's image exists in the supernal light, and it cannot be seen apart from that light. The world can be apprehended in the mode of supernal light—or not so apprehended—depending on the disposition and wisdom of the individual. This is apparent from saying 24: "There is light within a man of light, and he lights up all of the world. If he is not alight there is darkness." In saying 83 we read that the light within the images shall be revealed in an image of light, and that while the Father will be revealed, his image remains hidden in his light.

83 Jesus said: The images are revealed to people. The light within them is hidden in the image of the Father's light. He will be revealed. His image is hidden in his light.

84 Jesus said: You are pleased when you see your own likeness. When you see your images that came into being before you did, immortal and invisible images, how much can you bear?[96]

97 Adam is contrasted here with "you" (plural): the implied audience of these sayings. You are superior to Adam despite his creation by God, the source of enormous power and wealth. You will not die even though Adam did, and you are therefore of a different nature than Adam. If you are constituted as the Image of God, as saying 84 hints, then you pre-existed Adam, and like God's immortal Image you will live forever as the immortal Image does.

98 If Jesus lived an itinerant life, moving with his disciples from place to place irregularly, depending on occasional invitations and handouts for shelter and food, as the narrative gospels suggest, then saying 86 simply reflects the reality of his situation. In the canonical gospels, when "son of man" is used, sometimes it has a cosmic reference and other times it is simply a common idiom for "a person." We can be confident that here in Thomas 86 it is used as a common idiom, so the saying simply says that Jesus and people like Jesus have no fixed home.

99 How does a body depend on a body? By eating it. A human body eats animal bodies for food. Therefore, a soul, we hear, is wretched if it depends on a carnivorous mode of life. This saying does not attack "the body" per se, only a body that depends on meat for its sustenance. A vegetarian body is not one that depends on a body, so perhaps a soul dependent on it would not be wretched.

The Gospel of Thomas contains at least one more saying that also comes from a vegetarian perspective, saying 11c: "When you ate dead things, you made them alive. When you arrive into light, what will you do?" The reference to "when you ate dead things" is to the past and implies a changed present lifestyle wherein the people of the Gospel of Thomas no longer eat dead things. The process of digestion is what "you made them alive" means. Its reference to literal "dead things" consumed in the past contrasts with a future condition when an arrival into light will allow one, metaphorically, to eat "living things."

85 Jesus said: Adam came into being from enormous power and wealth, but he was never worthy of you, for had he been worthy of you he would not have died.[97]

86 Jesus said: Foxes have holes and birds have nests, but the son of man has no place to lay down his head and rest.[98]

87 Jesus said: Wretched is a body depending on a body, and wretched is a soul depending on these two.[99]

100 The word translated "messengers" can refer to what we call angels, for the Greek term *aggelos* means both. Prophets also, by definition, are messengers of God. What messengers give is information, so if they give you what is properly yours, you will receive information from God about your situation that you presently do not know but deserve to know. What will you give to the messengers/prophets/angels? If you have found some true knowledge of yourself and the world, this can be communicated back to God. Saying 3b implies this sort of mutuality of knowledge, for we hear: "When you understand yourselves you will be understood. And you will realize that you are Sons of the living Father."

However, the messengers and prophets might be human beings within the Christian movement. The Book of Acts contains accounts of early Christian prophets, as do the letters of Paul and the letters of John. If this is what the saying has in mind, then we should imagine social interaction between local people, represented by the audience of this saying, and itinerant people coming to them and expecting to exchange information for something else—perhaps the sustenance and shelter and respect they have a right to as Christian emissaries.

101 The fact that Jewish people washed dishes, food, and even their own bodies sometimes shocked other people in the ancient world. The evangelist Mark feels that he has to describe such curious customs to his readers and writes: "The Pharisees, and all the Jews, do not eat unless they thoroughly wash their hands, thus observing the tradition of the elders; and they do not eat anything from the market unless they wash it; and there are also many other traditions that they observe, the washing of cups, pots, and bronze kettles." (7:3–4).

It is reasonable to assume that neither Jesus nor his followers were interested in adopting the ritual cleanliness customs of the Judean elite. Jesus' associates were working-class people, and most of them were not Judeans but Galileans, whose religious practices and customs were not identical with those of the Judeans. Accordingly, saying 89 may have been spoken sarcastically to say that washing vessels at all is foolish, just as washing only the outside and not the inside is foolish.

88 Jesus said: The messengers are coming to you with the prophets, and they will give you what is properly yours. You then should give them what you have. Say to yourselves: "When will they come and take what is theirs?"[100]

89 Jesus said: Why wash the outside of the cup? Don't you know that the one who made the inside also made the outside?[101]

102 This saying is very similar to a comment about the Wisdom of God found in the Jewish book entitled *The Wisdom of Jesus ben Sirach* (also known as Ecclesiasticus): "Put your neck under her yoke, and let your souls receive instruction; it is to be found close by. See with your own eyes that I have labored but little and found for myself much serenity" (51:26–27). Here, in saying 90, a well-known expression appropriate to God's Wisdom is attributed to Jesus. In doing so, the Gospel of Thomas has Jesus speaking about himself as God's Wisdom.

"Rest" here seems to be a condition attainable in the present rather than an "eternal rest" to be obtained after death. In the Bible, the Letter to the Hebrews most prominently and repeatedly discusses "rest" as a reward for Christians, making the point that this kind of "rest" originates in the seventh-day rest of God in the week of the Beginning (Hebrews 4:8–12).

103 This is one of the sayings that most clearly express the unique perspectives of the Gospel of Thomas. The questioners represent those who would focus their attention on the person of Jesus himself, evidently assuming that what came to be known as "faith in Christ" is the proper essence of Christianity. In other words, they are seeking not to find the mystery of the Kingdom but the identity of Jesus himself.

They assume that Jesus primarily taught about himself. The Gospel of John shows him doing exactly that, for it is based on the principle that knowing who Jesus is (i.e., that he has come from the Father) is the essence of Christian faith and that Jesus continually tried to answer the demand "Tell us who you are so that we can believe in you." The Gospel of Thomas has no respect for this approach. In Thomas, when Jesus is asked about himself, he answers in terms of the whole world, deflecting attention from himself to the condition of reality.

90 Jesus said: Come to me. My yoke is easy. My mastery is gentle, and you will find rest for yourselves.[102]

91 They said to him: Tell us who you are so that we can believe in you. He replied: You analyze the appearance of the sky and the earth, but you don't recognize what is right in front of you, and you don't know the nature of the present time.[103]

104 Saying 92a implies the question "Seek what?" but Thomas is not going to give a clear answer. If seeking is the important thing, being given an answer cancels the process. You cannot "find" what you are given.

The Book of Proverbs, like other books featuring God's Wisdom, encourages readers to seek and find Wisdom. Sometimes Wisdom herself speaks in a manner similar to the manner of Jesus in the Gospel of Thomas. For example, she says: "those who seek me find me" (8:17) and "whoever finds me finds life" (8:35).

105 The missing element of this saying is preserved in Matthew 7:6: "Do not give what is holy to dogs; and do not throw your pearls before swine, or they will trample them underfoot." Each gospel features one half of a parallel structure proverb and is defective in the other half. Combined with the missing conclusion preserved by Matthew, Thomas 93 will read:

Do not give holy things to dogs,
for they might carry them off to the dung heap.
Do not give pearls to pigs,
for they might trample them underfoot.

The meaning of the parable is obvious and we have adopted it in English: "Don't throw your pearls before swine" is a commonplace expression.

106 This is a slightly fuller version of the saying found in Thomas 92a, and it is found in an even more thorough form in Matthew 7:7–8 and Luke 11:9–10. Like Thomas, Matthew doesn't specify what should be sought, although there Jesus does seems to have material benefits in mind, for he makes reference to the Father in heaven giving "good things to those who ask him." Luke is more precise and specifically identifies the Holy Spirit as that which the heavenly Father gives to those who ask (11:13). Thomas, of course, does not define what is to be found but leaves discovery to the reader.

92a Jesus said: Seek and you will find.

92b He said: In the past I did not answer the questions you asked. Now I am willing to answer, but you do not ask.[104]

93 Jesus said: Do not give holy things to dogs, for they might carry them off to the dung heap. Do not give pearls to pigs, for they might…[105]

94 Jesus said: Whoever seeks will find. Whoever knocks, it will be opened.[106]

107 The Gospel of Thomas is filled with enigmatic sayings that require introspection and a re-examination of the world, and yet it also states moral principles. Its ruling principle appears in saying 25: "Love your brother as your own soul. Protect him as you protect the pupil of your eye." Saying 95 follows logically from saying 25, for it clearly demands self-sacrificing generosity. Oddly enough, saying 95 appears to be in direct contradiction to one of the enigmatic commandments of saying 14a: "...if you give to charity you will damage your spirits." But, of course, any collection of remembered sayings will inevitably contain inconsistencies.

108 Both Matthew (13:33) and Luke (13:20–22) make use of this parable, each linking it directly to the parable of the mustard seed (Thomas saying 20). This is reasonable enough, for in both cases a parable speaks of something small (mustard seed, leavened dough) becoming something large: a huge plant, large loaves of bread. In the Gospel of Thomas, unlike the canonical gospels, the actual simile—what the Kingdom is like—is not the leavened dough but the woman. The Kingdom is not like a thing but like a person in action; the Kingdom is what someone does. When we look at the other parables in Thomas we find more often than not that the central simile likens the Kingdom to a person doing something, as in the next two of Thomas's sayings: 97, "The Kingdom of the Father is like a woman who..." and 98, "The Kingdom of the Father is like a man who..."

95 Jesus said: If you have some money, don't lend it out at interest but give it to someone who will not return it to you.[107]

96 Jesus said: The Kingdom of the Father is like a woman who took a little leaven and concealed it in dough. She made large loaves of bread. He who has ears let him hear.[108]

109 There is no reason to think that Jesus' parables were clearly understood by his audiences. Scholars in the past century have repeatedly concluded that his parables were startling and shocking, that they made unexpected connections and similes. Mark suggests that Jesus designed his parables to be riddles that his audiences could not understand (4:11–12). Today, though, the familiarity that they have for most Christians makes them seem to be quite clear. We think we know what the "mustard seed" represents, what the "sower" is allegorically sowing, what the prodigal son is like, and so forth. But Mark's author comments in his own voice about Jesus' technique to general audiences: "with many such parables he spoke the word to them, as they were able to hear it, but he did not speak to them except in parables" (4:33). Significantly, almost every saying in Mark's chapter 4 is from the Gospel of Thomas, as is virtually every single saying in Mark's Gospel that is called a parable there.

Through the discovery of the Gospel of Thomas we have, for the first time in nearly two thousand years, the opportunity to hear Jesus' voice "speaking in parables" without the intervening commentary of evangelists and preachers and church tradition. Thomas's saying 97 is one example. But for me to go further and offer any explanation of the parable's meaning would undermine its value as an almost unique example of what a parable of Jesus would have sounded like to an audience of his own time. If you find saying 97 shocking or puzzling or even flat-out incomprehensible, then you probably hear it as it was heard then.

97 Jesus said: The Kingdom of the Father is like
a woman who was carrying a jar full of grain.
As she walked along a handle of her jar broke off
and grain trickled out, but she didn't notice.
When she arrived in her house, she put the jar down
and found it empty.[109]

110 This parable, third in sequence and the second to be unique to the Gospel of Thomas (neither 97 nor 98 is found in any other text), does have a superficially obvious meaning: one should prepare in advance. That is the same message communicated by the adage found in Luke's Gospel 14:28: "for which of you, desiring to build a tower, does not first sit down and count the cost, whether he has enough to complete it?" Certainly "be prepared" is a good motto, but it is hardly something people haven't already thought of by themselves.

One must ask why this simile is presented the way it is. Why is the Kingdom of the Father like a man intending to kill a powerful man? Normally people do not assume that Jesus was fond of assassins, or that the Kingdom of the Father is correctly likened to their activities. Yet, elsewhere Jesus gives advice on the need to prepare in order to commit theft, as in saying 35. Jesus is almost always understood to be a man of peace, but that is an image Jesus rejected. We can see this from Thomas's saying 16a: "People think, perhaps, that I have come to throw peace upon the world. They don't know that I have come to throw disagreement upon the world, and fire, and sword, and struggle." We may think of Jesus as a man of peace, but he may have thought of himself in much more aggressive ways—as one who, for example, would cast fire upon the world (saying 10).

111 The commonly held notion that Jesus supported and valued family life is not in accord with the available evidence. The canonical gospels invariably show Jesus leaving his own family and commanding his disciples to leave theirs (e.g., Luke 9:57–62). One of the harsher sayings in the early traditions has him ordering his followers to hate their parents (saying 55 and Luke 14:26).

Saying 99 is one of the few bits of narrative in the collection. In Mark's version of saying 99 (3:31–35), it is clear that Jesus repudiates his biological family in favor of a new substitute family consisting of his followers who are obedient to God. This is not as clearly stated in the Thomas version, but it is certainly implied there. If "these here" are the ones who will enter the Kingdom, presumably Jesus' mother and brothers are "outsiders" who will not enter.

98 Jesus said: The Kingdom of the Father is like a man who intended to kill a powerful man. He drew out his sword in his own house and stabbed it into the wall to test his strength. Then he killed the powerful man.[110]

99 His disciples told him: Your brothers and your mother are standing outside. He responded: These here who do the will of my Father are my brothers and my mother. These are the ones who will enter the Kingdom of my Father.[111]

112 This familiar saying has a strange conclusion: "And give me what is mine." Perhaps the saying means that everything should be distributed to whomever it should properly be distributed to. In other words: "Give me what is mine, you what is yours, her what is hers, Caesar what is Caesar's, God what is God's, and so forth."

Or, to take another approach, the saying could specifically be about money, as the display of the coin would seem to indicate. Caesar (a symbol for Roman taxation authority) receives a certain amount of tax, but so does God, through the taxation authority of the Jerusalem temple. Saying 100 is reminiscent of saying 88, where "messengers" (angels) and "prophets" come to take what is theirs and give you what is yours. But what is that? And what does Jesus expect to be given? Thomas's Gospel is silent on those questions.

113 This saying is a version of saying 55, a "hard" saying, wherein Jesus orders his followers to hate their fathers and their mothers: "He who doesn't hate his father and mother cannot be a disciple of mine." Saying 101a softens this unambiguous command by making it much more ambiguous, for the "as I do" clauses include a command to love one's parents as Jesus loves his.

❖ "In contrast to the Synoptic Sayings source, the Gospel of Thomas proposes an interpretation of the sayings of Jesus which has no futuristic eschatological component, but instead proclaims the presence of divine wisdom as the true destiny of human existence. The message of the Gospel of Thomas is fundamentally esoteric and is directed to a limited group of elect people."

—Helmut Koester, *History and Literature of Early Christianity*, p. 153

100 They showed Jesus a gold coin and said: Caesar's agents demand that we pay his taxes. He replied: Give to Caesar what is Caesar's. Give to God what is God's. And give me what is mine.[112]

101a Jesus said: Anyone who doesn't hate his father and his mother as I do cannot be a disciple of mine. And anyone who doesn't love his father and mother as I do cannot be a disciple of mine.

101b My mother has…but true she gave me life.[113]

114 Saying 102 clearly expresses a negative attitude toward Pharisees and, to a limited degree, gives a reason for that attitude, taking it for granted that Pharisees do in fact have possession of something necessary to a reader of the Gospel of Thomas and that they will not make it available even though they have no interest in it. Almost exactly the same complaint is made in saying 39a: "The Pharisees and the scribes have taken the keys to knowledge and have hidden them. They did not go in, and they did not permit those desiring to go in to enter." But what are the "keys of knowledge" that allow one to enter? Where? We are not told here, but in Matthew's Gospel the term "keys" symbolizes the power to decide legal cases so as to create precedents regarding what is required by the law of God and what is not allowed—decisions that are binding both on earth and in heaven (Matthew 16:19). Accordingly, human legal authorities can make decisions that count as God's law. If, then, these are the "keys" that Thomas's Gospel mentions, then the knowledge in question is legal knowledge, the particular specialty of Pharisees.

115 As sayings 65 and 98 do, this saying encourages preparation and planning, and it evidences a cultural background replete with violence and threat. The occupation of Galilee by Judean forces under the Maccabees around 104 B.C., followed by the Roman takeover in 63 B.C., followed by the reign of Herod, who died circa 5 B.C., was a period of great social change and oppression, and it did not grow more peaceful during Jesus' lifetime. Indeed, social disruptions due to occupation and excessive taxation led to the great Jewish revolt of the 60s A.D. that culminated in the destruction of the Jerusalem Temple in 70 A.D. Bandits and violence and assassinations were part of life throughout the period.

102 Jesus said: Woe to the Pharisees. Like a dog dozing in a food trough for cattle, they neither eat nor do they let the cattle eat.[114]

103 Jesus said: Blessed is one who knows where (or when) bandits are going to attack, so that he can prepare, assemble his forces, and arm himself before the bandits enter.[115]

116 In light of Thomas's ideology and its symbolic vocabulary, saying 104 makes reasonably good sense. Jesus is asked to engage in the religious activities he condemns in saying 14a, where he says: "If you fast you will bring sin to yourselves, and if you pray you will be condemned, and if you give to charity you will damage your spirits." Saying 14 does not explain why religious activities give rise to such difficulties, but saying 104 does. The problem is that prayer and fasting are modes of repentance, and repentance presupposes sins that are in need of repentance. Jesus, in saying 104, implicitly denies any sin and therefore has no need to pray and fast.

The bridal suite seems to be a symbol of unity, where "the two become one." When the groom leaves the bridal suite, the two are no longer one. So Thomas's insistence on unification, best seen through saying 22, has a symbolic application here. Those who are unified, solitary, and "one" are without sin and have no need to fast and pray. But if they leave the bridal suite, and so have become two, then presumably they will find fasting and prayer necessary. Note that "they" rather than "you" is the form used here, so that Jesus implicitly is speaking about people outside the immediate audience of the saying. Those who are like the infant of seven days resting in the Beginning have no need of acts of repentance.

117 According to the Gospels, Jesus' father was not a man married to Jesus' mother, and in all of the New Testament, Jesus is called "son of Joseph" only twice, both instances occurring in the Gospel of John. Later and not very reliable Jewish texts speak of his father being Pantherus, a soldier, and speak of his mother as having been impregnated against her will. All of this adds up to the possibility that Jesus was not of legitimate birth; for such people at that time, name-calling would not be unexpected.

Here Jesus claims to know who his father is, as well as his mother's identity. Perhaps his statement is intended to refute intimations of illegitimacy.

104 They said to Jesus: Come, let's pray today; let's fast. Jesus responded: What sin have I committed? How have I been overcome? Rather, when the groom leaves the bridal suite, then they should fast and pray.[116]

105 Jesus said: One who knows his father and his mother will be called the son of a whore.[117]

118 One might paraphrase saying 106 thus: "When you make the two into one, you will be called fully human." Thomas's frequently reiterated theme of unification, of oneness, of merging the two into one seems to have as its postulated goal the attainment of a fully human condition by people who have not yet gained that status.

This saying is a variation on saying 48: "If two can make peace between themselves in a single house, they can say to a mountain, 'Move!' and it will move." If we combine the ideas in these two sayings, then "make peace between themselves" and "become one" would be equivalent phrases. It would follow then that the Gospel of Thomas speaks of a down-to-earth union of wills between people determined to get along together. At that point, the sayings declare, anything is possible, and, metaphorically, mountains will move.

119 In this version of the famous "lost sheep" parable, the sheep is the largest and most favored. This is also the pattern of the parable of the pearl (saying 76a), in which a merchant gives everything up to get the one great pearl. It is also the pattern found in the parable of the fish (saying 8), in which a fisherman keeps the one fine fish and discards a pile of trivial fish. As the parables of the leaven (saying 96) and the mustard seed (saying 20) both seem to use the image of a small thing growing huge, so the parables of the fish, pearl, and sheep seem to use the image of a great thing attained by putting aside lesser things.

❖ "Its origin and development may be obscure, the processes of its composition present many problems, even the interpretation of some of the sayings may at times be difficult; the final solution of these and other problems lies still in the future. But that the discovery of this document is an event of the first importance there can be no doubt."

—Robert McL. Wilson, *Studies in the Gospel of Thomas* (London: Mowbray & Co., 1960), p. 153

106 Jesus said: When you make the two into one, you will be called sons of men. When you say, "Move, mountain!" it will move.[118]

107 Jesus said: The Kingdom is like a shepherd with one hundred sheep. One of those sheep, the largest, wandered off. He left the ninety-nine others behind and went looking for the other one until he found it. Having exhausted himself, he said to the sheep, "I love you more than the other ninety-nine."[119]

120 Jesus, as Wisdom, communicates through wise sayings and parables, as does the wise man, according to Ben Sirach 39:6: "If it is the will of the great Lord he will be filled with a spirit of intelligence; then he will pour forth wise sayings of his own." One who seeks Wisdom "preserves the sayings of famous men and penetrates the intricacies of parables. He investigates the hidden meaning of proverbs and knows his way among riddles" (39:2–3). It is hard to imagine a more apt description of one who seeks to "interpret the meaning of these sayings" in Thomas.

In sayings 108 and 13, those who meditate on the Gospel of Thomas are drinking from Wisdom's fountain. "Drinking" is done by means of investigating and penetrating the intricacies of parables and proverbs, as is discussed in Thomas's prologue and in saying 1. He who does this becomes as Jesus is. Implicitly, he will be capable of pouring forth wise sayings of his own through a spirit of Wisdom. We hear in saying 108 that he will have revealed to him the things that are hidden, and that brings us back in Thomas's structure to the sayings that begin the text, especially sayings 5 and 6. Thomas, as it reaches its conclusion, reaches back to its own beginning.

121 This saying has been garbled in transmission, for there really is no featured character who does anything either intelligently or unintelligently. Rather, the first two characters act rationally enough in light of the fact that they are ignorant of the treasure, and the third character is just lucky. His lending money at interest may be a mark against him in the Thomasine context, because saying 95 unambiguously advises against the practice.

108 Jesus said: He who drinks from my mouth will become like I am, and I will become he. And the hidden things will be revealed to him.[120]

109 Jesus said: The Kingdom is like a man with a treasure of which he is unaware hidden in his field. He died and left the field to his son. His son knew nothing about it and, having received the field, sold it. The new owner came and, while plowing, found the treasure. He began to lend money at interest to anybody he wished.[121]

122 The pair of sayings 80 and 81 sounds very much like saying 110:

> 80. Jesus said: Whoever has come to know the world has found the body. Whoever has found the body, the world is not worthy of him.
> 81. Jesus said: Whoever has become rich should rule. Whoever has power should renounce it.

In all cases, finding the world is commended but not defined. The consequence of finding the world is becoming rich, and the stage beyond becoming rich is renouncing power or renouncing the world. Poverty, in saying 3b, represents the state of people who have not known themselves and, by reference to 3a, also the state of people who have not found the Kingdom present in the world. Riches, of course, represent the opposite case: those who have discovered the Kingdom's presence.

123 This saying needs to be understood in combination with saying 11:

> 11a. This sky will cease to be, and the sky above it will cease to be.
> 11b. The dead do not live, and the living will not die.
> 11c. When you ate dead things, you made them alive. [When you arrive into light, what will you do?]
> 11d. When you were one, you became two. When you become two, what will you do?

I have placed the second clause of the first question in brackets because there may be a more original version of this saying in Hippolytus' *Refutatio* V, 8.32, which preserves a parallelism lost in Thomas's version: "You who have eaten of dead things and have brought them to life, what will you do if you eat living things?" Quite probably the answer was so obvious to a scribe who copied Thomas that he gave the answer as the question: "What will you do if you eat living things?" Why, "you will come into the light!" Living by the living and coming into the light may have been equivalent expressions.

110 Jesus said: Whoever has found the world and become rich should renounce the world.[122]

111a Jesus said: The earth and sky will roll up right in front of you. Anyone living from the living will not die.[123]

111b Doesn't Jesus say that the world is not worthy of one who finds himself?

124 This saying gives no precedence to soul or to flesh; they appear to be equivalent in value. In real life, the soul and the flesh are indeed interdependent. The present saying may make the point that ideally the two would be mutually independent and it is unfortunate that they aren't. Saying 112 follows rationally in sequence after saying 111, which speaks of "living from the living" in apparent contrast to living from what is dead. Differently phrased, being a "body depending on a body" and "woe to the soul dependent on the flesh" may have such behavior in mind. Living on the living would be the vegetarian alternative to the carnivorous behavior condemned in saying 87.

❖ "The Gospel of Thomas has proved to be a gold mine of comparative material and new information. Thomas has forty-seven parallels to Mark, forty parallels to Q, seventeen to Matthew, four to Luke, and five to John. These numbers include sayings that have been counted twice. About sixty-five sayings or parts of sayings are unique to Thomas. (Complex sayings in Thomas, as in the other gospels, are often made up of more than one saying, so that the total number of individual items in Thomas exceeds one hundred and fourteen.) These materials, which many scholars take to represent a tradition quite independent of the other gospels, provide what scientists call a 'control group' for the analysis of sayings and parables that appear in other gospels."

—Robert W. Funk, Roy W. Hoover, and the Jesus Seminar,
The Five Gospels: The Search for the Authentic Words of Jesus, p. 15

112 Jesus said: Woe to the flesh dependent on the soul; woe to the soul dependent on the flesh.[124]

125 Saying 113 is probably the last in the sequence of sayings that made up the original Gospel of Thomas, for saying 114 seems to have been added later. Saying 113 is an important summation of the worldview reflected in many of Thomas's sayings, which is that the Kingdom is here now, and people must learn to discern it rather than waiting for some cosmic miracle to bring the Kingdom down to earth.

Thomas's Gospel does not have very much structure to it, but it has a little. The prologue and first saying introduce the work. Jesus' first saying, number 2 in the list, raises the often repeated theme "seek and you will find" and defines the sort of seeking required as an internal quest with emotionally powerful results. Saying 3 follows with a "topic paragraph" outlining the main points: "The Kingdom is within you and outside of you. Know yourselves!" along with a critique of the position that the Kingdom is out there somewhere waiting to arrive in the future. Saying 113 brings the circle back to its beginning and reiterates the strong statement of saying 3: the Kingdom of the Father is already here.

As saying 3 criticizes leaders who put the Kingdom out there in the sky or beyond the sea, so saying 113 by its misguided opening question implicitly criticizes the branch of Christianity (later to become the Church) that expects the Kingdom to arrive in the future.

Thomas's sayings are often polemical in a similar question-and-answer pattern, most frequently labeling the questioners as "his disciples." There are two principal varieties of misguided questions:

Questions regarding the end:

18. Tell us about our end. What will it be?
51. When will the dead rest? When will the new world arrive?
113. When is the Kingdom coming?

Questions regarding the nature of Jesus:

24. Show us the place you are for it is essential for us to seek it.
37. When will you appear to us? When will we see you?

(continued on page 138)

113 They asked him: When is the Kingdom coming? He replied: It is not coming in an easily observable manner. People will not be saying, "Look, it's over here" or "Look, it's over there." Rather, the Kingdom of the Father is already spread out on the earth, and people aren't aware of it.[125]

43. Who are you to say these things to us?
52. Twenty-four prophets spoke to Israel and they all spoke of you.
91. Tell us who you are so that we can believe in you.

Thomas's Gospel, through these questions and Jesus' answers, criticizes two of the "rocks" on which the later Christian churches based their faith: the idea that the Kingdom will come in the future and the idea that Jesus himself is the central aspect of the religion that he founded. Thomas's Gospel teaches that while Jesus is a teacher of great importance, his teachings are the important factor, not his person.

126 The final saying, 114, was added to the text of Thomas at some later date. Not only is it a saying that repels the modern reader, it also spoils the nice symmetry between saying 3 at the beginning and saying 113 at the conclusion. Naturally there would be no easier place to add a saying to a list than at the end. It combines in an odd way a pro-woman perspective, for Jesus rejects the males-only view put into the mouth of Peter, with an anti-woman perspective, for women are to make themselves men. Probably that strange notion has to do with the idea that "woman" represents passions and "man" represents reason, in accordance with some of the symbolic language of ancient philosophy. In any event, saying 114 is contradicted by saying 22, which requires the union of the sexes rather than preference for one over the other.

114 Simon Peter said to them: Mary should leave us because women are not worthy of the life. Jesus responded: Look, I'll lead her in order to make her male so that she can become a living spirit as you males are. For each woman who makes herself male will enter into the Kingdom of Heaven.[126]

Suggested Readings and Resources

Bloom, Harold. "A Reading," in *The Gospel of Thomas: The Hidden Sayings of Jesus*, edited by Marvin Meyer. New York: HarperSanFrancisco, 1992.

Cameron, Ron. *The Other Gospels: Non-Canonical Gospel Texts*. Philadelphia: Westminster Press, 1982.

Davies, Stevan. *The Gospel of Thomas and Christian Wisdom*. New York: Seabury Press, 1983.

Funk, Robert W., Roy W. Hoover, and the Jesus Seminar. *The Five Gospels: The Search for the Authentic Words of Jesus*. Sonoma, Calif.: Polebridge Press, 1993.

Koester, Helmut. *History and Literature of Early Christianity*. Philadelphia: Fortress Press, 1982.

———. "Introduction to the Gospel of Thomas," in *The Nag Hammadi Library in English*, edited by James Robinson, 3rd ed. New York: HarperSanFrancisco, 1988.

Layton, Bentley. *The Gnostic Scriptures: A New Translation with Annotations and Introductions.* New York: Doubleday, 1987.

Merillat, Herbert Christian. *The Gnostic Apostle Thomas.* Philadelphia: Xlibris, 1997.

Meyer, Marvin, ed. *The Gospel of Thomas: The Hidden Sayings of Jesus*. New York: HarperSanFrancisco, 1992.

Patterson, Stephen J. *The Gospel of Thomas and Jesus.* Sonoma, Calif.: Polebridge Press, 1993.

———. "Introduction to the Gospel of Thomas," in *Q-Thomas Reader*, edited by John Kloppenborg. Sonoma, Calif.: Polebridge Press, 1990.

Valantasis, Richard. *The Gospel of Thomas*. London and New York: Routledge, 1997.